Anne Morrow Lindbergh

Twayne's United States Authors Series

Kenneth E. Eble, Editor

University of Utah

TUSAS 539

ANNE MORROW LINDBERGH, C. 1970
(1906–   )
Photograph by Richard W. Brown

Anne Morrow Lindbergh

By David Kirk Vaughan

Air Force Institute of Technology

Twayne Publishers
A Division of G. K. Hall & Co. • Boston

Anne Morrow Lindbergh

David Kirk Vaughan

Copyright 1988 by G. K. Hall & Co.
All rights reserved.
Published by Twayne Publishers
A Division of G. K. Hall & Co.
70 Lincoln Street
Boston, Massachusetts 02111

Copyediting supervised by Barbara Sutton.
Book production by Patricia D'Agostino.
Book design by Barbara Anderson.

Typeset in 11 pt. Garamond
by Compset, Inc., Beverly, Massachusetts.

Printed on permanent/durable acid-free paper
and bound in the United States of America.

Library of Congress Cataloging-in-Publication Data

Vaughan, David Kirk.
    Anne Morrow Lindbergh / by David Kirk Vaughan.
        p.   cm.—(Twayne's United States authors series ; TUSAS 539)
    Bibliography: p.
    Includes index.
    ISBN 0-8057-7520-X (alk. paper)
    1. Lindbergh, Anne Morrow, 1906–   —Criticism and interpretation.
    I. Title. II. Series.
    PS3523.I516Z9   1988
    818'.5209—dc19   88-6060
                                                                        CIP

Contents

About the Author

David Kirk Vaughan received a B.S. in engineering sciences at the U.S. Air Force Academy in 1962 and a Ph.D. in English language and literature from the University of Washington in 1974. While serving in the U.S. Air Force, he flew a variety of cargo, refueling, and training aircraft. He taught English at the Air Force Academy and the University of Maine and is currently on the faculty of the Department of Communication and Organizational Sciences at the Air Force Institute of Technology, Wright-Patterson Air Force Base, Dayton, Ohio.

Preface

Anne Morrow Lindbergh presents a number of unique challenges to anyone who would undertake a study of her published writings. She is at once one of the most self-revealing writers of this century and yet she has avoided the public eye. All of her books are clearly biographical in nature, but she herself is sensitive to intrusions into her personal life. Married to one of this century's most widely recognized legitimate heroes, she nevertheless managed to maintain her own discrete artistic vision, readily admitting that her partnership with her famous husband led her into life experiences that simultaneously frightened her, exhilarated her, and molded her aesthetic outlook. Lindbergh's travels with her husband brought her into contact with a world she had never previously encountered, the world of physical action, technology, and machinery. While the efforts required to adjust to the pace of her husband's activities were demanding, she was unwilling to make her life easier by remaining at home while he engaged in his travels. Although her willing cooperation in the activities of his world interfered with her personal life and professional goals, she accepted these interruptions and integrated them into her creative work.

Surprisingly, critical evaluation of Anne Morrow Lindbergh's written work is almost nonexistent. Practically the only commentary about her thirteen books of memoirs, poetry, essays, and fiction is in the form of book reviews issued at the time of publication. Only the French writer Antoine de Saint-Exupéry, of all her readers, was able to appreciate Lindbergh's style and subject and to see it as part of an integral, unified artistic expression. Because Anne Morrow Lindbergh participated so successfully in both the active, technical world of her husband and in her own world of philosophical expression, it has been difficult to assess her full achievement. Yet a continuity can be established between her life as an aviator and her life as a writer—her dedication to communication.

This dedication is evident in the seriousness with which she accepted her duties as a radio operator on their 1931 and 1933 continent-spanning flights. While her husband was in the front seat of their Lockheed Sirius monoplane, directing their progress across the desolate, uninhabited landscape of northern Canada and Alaska, she was hard at work in the rear seat of their two-place cockpit, concentrating intently on maintaining communications with radio stations along their route. Painstakingly operating the radio, transmitting and receiving messages in Morse code, physically winding their aerial in and out after takeoff and before landing, she obtained weather conditions and landing information essential to their safe arrival. In addition to marking their own progress along their intended route of flight, she related their movements to the outside world by passing along hourly position reports, information vitally necessary for rescuers if they were forced to land unexpectedly. She continued her communications role even after their world-circling flights ended, for her writings consistently mark her progress through life, a progress closely linked to that of her husband. Even though this movement is more often of a spiritual rather than physical nature, her purpose is twofold: to measure her own progress, and to tell others of that progress.

While it is a well-established truth that knowledge of a writer's life sheds light on the meanings of a writer's works, it is an absolute requirement in the case of Anne Morrow Lindbergh, for her works were never intended as allegorical or restated adaptations of her life presented in fictional form. In every one of her works, even the first travel narrative, the motive is one of revelation of self, of working toward a clearer perception of how one should live one's life. Lindbergh is a philosopher at heart, and not a writer of novels or poetry, a fact that becomes evident as one reviews her total creative output. Her philosophical inclination also explains why she so often builds her essays upon the thoughts of earlier philosopher-writers like Saint-Exupéry and Rainer Maria Rilke.

Because Lindbergh's writings are so closely linked to the events of her life, it is especially important that they be examined in the light of those events. Fortunately, she has made a wealth of biographical material available, at least for the years prior to the end of World War II. These materials are her diaries and letters, which she published from 1972 through 1980; in addition to serving as unique literary documents in their own right, these five volumes also provide detailed accounts of the major events in the lives of the Lindbergh family from 1927 through 1944. Although these works were the last published, they were compiled early in her life, and are discussed in connection with the biographical details in the first chapters of this study.

For ease of reference Lindbergh's published works are identified throughout this study by the following two-letter codes: *North to the Orient (NO), Listen! the Wind (LW), The Wave of the Future (WF), The Steep Ascent (SA), Gift from the Sea (GS), The Unicorn and Other Poems (UP), Dearly Beloved (DB), Earth Shine (ES), Bring Me a Unicorn (BU), Hour of Gold, Hour of Lead (HG), Locked Rooms and Open Doors (LR), The Flower and the Nettle (FN), War Within and Without (WW).* Page numbers cited in the text in parentheses are those of the first trade editions. Page numbers may differ noticeably from popular book club editions of the volumes of the diaries and letters. Other parenthetical page references are to publications given full identification in the bibliography.

In this study the Lindbergh surname is usually used in reference to the central figure, Anne Morrow Lindbergh; occasionally, however, it is used in reference to Charles Lindbergh whenever the discussion focuses on his activities. I have tried to avoid confusion by clearly identifying which individual is under consideration. Because the Lindbergh name identifies two exceptionally well known individuals, there does not seem to be any way to avoid the occasional transfer of reference.

Helpful assistance in this study was provided by Judith A. Schiff, chief research archivist, and the staff of the Sterling Collection at the Yale University Library. Additional assistance came from members of the Princeton University Library and the library of the National Air and Space Museum, Smithsonian Institution, Washington, D.C. Dorothy Green and the staff of the Sophia Smith Collection, Smith College library, were especially cooperative. The Office of the Dean, College of Arts and Sciences, University of Maine, provided grant money through the Faculty Development Fund to support visits to the libraries mentioned above. I am also grateful to Professor Burton Hatlen, Chair of the Department of English at the University of Maine, for supporting the preparation of the initial draft of this study. Special thanks go to Richard Brucher, of the University of Maine, for his helpful suggestions. Valuable editorial assistance was provided by Kenneth Eble, Twayne field editor; thanks also go to Athenaide Dallett and Liz Traynor, of Twayne's Boston office, for their understanding and persistent support.

I would like to thank my Maryland friends Jim Tice, Amy Boxwell, Vera Rollo, and Bill and Bonnie Brose for providing the impetus to begin this project, and also Winterport, Maine, resident Ray Hills, whose friendly queries provided the best kind of encouragement along the road to completion. I would like to thank my wife, Francoise, for her patience and interest in the project. Last but certainly not least, I must thank Anne Morrow Lindbergh for generously accommodating my inquiries.

David Kirk Vaughan

Air Force Institute of Technology

Acknowledgments

Photograph of Anne Morrow Lindbergh, c. 1970, by Richard W. Brown, courtesy of the Smith College Archives, Smith College.

Excerpts from *Bring Me a Unicorn,* copyright © 1971, 1972 by Anne Morrow Lindbergh; *Hour of Gold, Hour of Lead,* copyright © 1973 by Anne Morrow Lindbergh; *Locked Rooms and Open Doors,* copyright © 1974 by Anne Morrow Lindbergh; *The Flower and the Nettle,* copyright © 1976 by Anne Morrow Lindbergh; *War Within and Without,* copyright © 1980 by Anne Morrow Lindbergh; *North to the Orient,* copyright © 1935, 1963 by Anne Morrow Lindbergh; *Listen! The Wind,* copyright © 1938, 1966 by Anne Morrow Lindbergh; *The Wave of the Future,* copyright © 1940 by Anne Morrow Lindbergh; *The Steep Ascent,* copyright © 1944 by Anne Morrow Lindbergh; *Dearly Beloved,* copyright by Anne Morrow Lindbergh; and *Earth Shine,* copyright © 1966, 1969 by Anne Morrow Lindbergh. Reprinted by permission of Harcourt Brace Jovanovich, Inc.

Excerpts from *Gift from the Sea,* copyright © 1955 by Anne Morrow Lindbergh and *The Unicorn and Other Poems* copyright © 1956 by Anne Morrow Lindbergh. Reprinted by permission of Pantheon Books, a Division of Random House, Inc., New York.

Excerpts from *Gift from the Sea, Bring me a Unicorn, Dearly Beloved* and *Earth Shine* courtesy of Anne Morrow Lindbergh and Chatto & Windus, Inc., London.

Chronology

1906   Born Anne Spencer Morrow, 22 June, in Englewood, New Jersey; second daughter and second child of Dwight Morrow and Elizabeth Cutter Morrow.

1927   Charles Augustus Lindbergh, Jr., flies the Atlantic Ocean to Paris, 20–21 May. Anne Morrow meets CAL 21 December in Mexico City at the home of her father who is serving as ambassador to Mexico.

1928   Graduates from Smith College, Northampton, Massachusetts, June.

1929   Marries CAL, Englewood, New Jersey, 27 May. Flight with CAL and Juan and Betty Trippe to Central and South America, September–October.

1930   First son, Charles Augustus, Jr., born 22 June.

1931   Earns pilot license, May; July–October flies with CAL to Canada, Alaska, Russia, Japan, China. Death of father, Dwight Morrow, October.

1932   Kidnapping and death of son Charles, 1 March. Second son, Jon, born 16 August.

1933   July–September flies with CAL to Greenland, Iceland, Scandinavia, Europe, Africa, South America.

1934   Bruno Hauptmann arrested and charged with the murder of the Lindbergh baby, September.

1935   Trial of Bruno Hauptmann, January–February. *North to the Orient* published, August. Lindberghs move to England, December.

1937   February–March flies with CAL from England to Italy and India. Third son, Land, born 12 May.

1938   Lindberghs move to Illiec, France, June. *Listen! the Wind!* published, September.

1939   Lindberghs return to the United States, April. Antoine de Saint-Exupéry visits the Lindberghs, 5–7 August.

1940   *The Wave of the Future* published, October. First daughter, Anne, born 20 October.

1940–1941   CAL gives numerous addresses urging nonintervention in the war in Europe.

1942   CAL serves as aviation consultant and test pilot with Ford Motor Company aircraft plant, Detroit, April; Lindberghs move to Bloomfield Hills, Michigan, July. Fourth son, Scott, born 12 August.

1944   *The Steep Ascent* published, February. CAL involved in test-flying duties in Pacific theater, April–October. AML establishes Lindbergh residence in Connecticut, September–October.

1945   Second daughter, Reeve, born 20 October.

1948   Publication of several essays describing European postwar recovery.

1954   Death of Evangeline Lodge Lindbergh, mother of CAL.

1955   Death of mother, Elizabeth Cutter Morrow.

1955   *Gift from the Sea.*

1956   *The Unicorn and Other Poems.*

1962   *Dearly Beloved.*

1969   *Earth Shine.*

1974   Death of Charles Lindbergh, Maui, Hawaii, 26 August.

1972–1980   Publication of diaries and letters in five volumes: *Bring Me a Unicorn,* 1972; *Hour of Gold, Hour of Lead,* 1973; *Locked Rooms and Open Doors,* 1974; *The Flower and the Nettle,* 1976; *War Within and Without,* 1980.

Chapter One
The Early Years

It is not surprising that the subject matter and style of Anne Morrow Lindbergh's writings reflect conservative middle-class values, for the most part, for those values were thoroughly instilled in her during her childhood years in the Morrow household. She was born into a household whose family fortunes were rapidly rising. Her father, Dwight Whitney Morrow, came from a middle-class background and soon established himself as a successful and valued member of the J. P. Morgan financial firm. Her mother, Elizabeth Reeve Cutter, was an industrious and active woman and a strong supporter of education and social issues. As Morrow's standing increased in the Morgan firm, the Morrow family was able to move in the upper levels of society, and their children were able to benefit from travel abroad and education at the country's most prestigious institutions.

Anne Spencer Morrow was the second of four children. She was born at the Morrow house in Englewood, New Jersey, 22 June 1906. There were two other daughters, Elisabeth, the eldest, born in 1904, and Constánce, the youngest, born in 1913. The one son in the household, Dwight, Junior, followed Anne by two years. The senior Morrow had met his bride-to-be in 1893, when he was a student at Amherst College and she was attending a girl's preparatory school nearby. Dwight and Elizabeth were married in Cleveland on 16 June 1903, and Anne was born almost exactly three years later. Dwight and Elizabeth Morrow were formidable models of learning and industry; the achievements of both were exceptional, and it is not surprising that they became models that were almost too successful for successful imitation.

Dwight and Elizabeth Morrow

Dwight Morrow was the fourth of eight children born to a West Virginia schoolteacher and his wife; Morrow was born two years after his father had been appointed president of Marshall College, Huntington, West Virginia. Morrow was eager for an education, but was not initially successful in his search to obtain it; he was refused admission at West Point, was unhappy at Washington and Jefferson, and was finally able to reach his goal at Amherst, Massachusetts, from which he graduated in 1895, having been elected class orator. He had also made friends with a classmate named Calvin Coolidge. He attended Columbia Law School and completed his legal schooling in 1899.

After his marriage he quickly advanced in his legal positions, primarily because he was an energetic and indefatigable worker. In 1914 he joined the prestigious banking firm of J. P. Morgan and Company, becoming a partner in the firm in July of that year. When war broke out in Europe, the J. P. Morgan firm was appointed agent for both the French and British governments, and Morrow became increasingly involved in foreign financial affairs. In the spring of 1918 he traveled to Europe as a member of the Allied Maritime Transport Council, in which capacity he met leading members of the international finance community. He also visited the Allied Military headquarters in France, where he met General Pershing. Impressed with Morrow, Pershing offered him a commission in the army, which Morrow politely refused.

After the armistice, Morrow supported Calvin Coolidge's campaign for the presidency, hoping to become involved in politics. In 1921 he was offered the presidency of Yale University; he declined the offer but later expressed regret at doing so. Still a partner in the J. P. Morgan firm, he visited Cuba in an attempt to assist negotiations pertaining to Cuban sugar. When Calvin Coolidge became president in August of 1923 after the sudden death of Warren G. Harding, Morrow expected to be asked to participate in government service. But for several months no call came from his former Amherst classmate. In the fall of 1925 Coolidge asked him to be a member of the Aircraft Inquiry Board, which Coolidge established in response to Brigadier General Billy Mitchell's claims that the government was not responsive to the needs of military aviation. This board, which eventually became known as the "Morrow Board," diplomatically responded to the Mitchell complaints. Morrow's efforts were eventually rewarded by his appointment as ambassador to Mexico in July 1927.

Morrow remained as ambassador to Mexico until 1929, but maintained an interest in Latin American political affairs. In January 1930 Herbert Hoover interviewed him about a possible position in the president-elect's cabinet. Preferring his work in Mexico, Morrow stayed on as ambassador. From January to April of 1930 Morrow was temporarily detailed to work with the American contingent at the London Conference on Naval Disarmament, where his diplomacy and tact were instrumental in achieving a degree of international agreement.

On 3 December 1930 he entered Congress as a senator from New Jersey, elected to fill an unexpired term and also elected to fill a new six-year term beginning in March 1931. But he died unexpectedly in his sleep early in the morning of 5 October 1931, of a cerebral hemorrhage. He was fifty-eight years old. His death occurred while the Lindberghs were visiting China on their flight to the Far East.

His death dealt Anne Morrow Lindbergh a severe blow, for he was the first and most lasting influence on her career as a writer. She was especially impressed with his philosophic outlook and his natural inclination toward conciliation, evidenced repeatedly in numerous international conferences in which he was involved. A moderate by nature, he invariably applied his careful, rational approach to problem solving, whether on a local, national, or international level. Morrow achieved substantial success as a mediator in international disputes, especially in the London Conference of 1930, and it was in much the same spirit that Lindbergh envisioned herself in the writing of *The Wave of the Future* and her postwar essays. In the summer of 1940, when Lindbergh and her husband were involved in their noninterventionist activities, she recalled her father's viewpoint, nearly ten years after his death: "I wonder where Daddy would stand? Probably behind the [America First] committee et al. And yet he was, among those idealists, very practical, intensely practical—that was his great gift. The combination of vision and practicality" (*WW*, 97–98). A kindred spirit of vision and practicality can be found in *Gift from the Sea* and *Dearly Beloved.*

If Elizabeth Cutter Morrow was required by social custom to accompany her dynamic husband on his national and international travels and to maintain the home in a fashion appropriate to the family's steadily rising social status, these constraints did not limit her own personal interests and activities. Although she was occupied initially with the upbringing of the four Morrow children and the management of the household, her social calendar was always filled, especially after the death of her husband.

Elizabeth Morrow had been raised in the Cleveland, Ohio, area and returned there to teach in a private school after she completed her education at Smith College in 1895. In 1899 she and her sister traveled to Europe for two years, where she studied at the Sorbonne and in Florence. She graduated with distinction from Smith College and maintained her ties to that institution throughout her life, as did her daughter Anne years later. Mrs. Morrow was the first woman chairman of the Board of Trustees of Smith College, and served briefly as interim president of the college in 1939. She also established a poetry library and a house at Smith College (*BU*, 79).

Anne Morrow Lindbergh's numerous references to her mother's activities in her letters and diaries testify to Mrs. Morrow's energetic pace and event-filled social calendar. Although Mrs. Morrow's activities may have been partly the result of a need to fill the void caused by the death of her husband, it is also evident that she too was an energetic and dynamic individual. While Lindbergh was deeply influenced by her mother, that influence was reflected less in the area of writing than in her social outlook. Lindbergh eventually overcame her initial feelings of awe at her mother's activities after she became successful as a writer. As Lindbergh points out in *Bring Me a Unicorn*, hers was an education-oriented family, and one in which education was intended for public as well as personal good (*BU*, xvi). Both parents provided practical evidence of this philosophy.

The Morrow family made their primary home in Englewood, New Jersey, where they lived after the marriage of Dwight and Elizabeth in 1903 until well after World War II. Englewood at that time offered a small-town environment in a community not yet linked directly to New York City. The first Morrow home, a rental, was located on Spring Lane. Their next home was located on Palisade Avenue, into which the family moved in May 1909. It was the house in which Anne was raised. In the fall of 1928 the Morrow family moved again, this time into Next Day Hill, a house that had been built according to their design. The architect for the house was Chester Aldrich, an old friend of the Morrows; he also designed the Morrow summer home on North Haven Island, in Penobscot Bay, off the coast of Maine. That house was completed by the summer of 1928. Anne spent part of the summer of that year at North Haven; it was the one residence that continually offered her a sense of rest and safety. She and Charles returned to it often over the next fifteen years. It was especially important to her as a refuge from 1932 to 1935.

After receiving preliminary education at Miss Chapin's school, Anne Morrow entered Smith College in the fall of 1924, following in the footsteps of her mother and her older sister. Her academic career there was generally undistinguished until she began to achieve success in her writing classes. In a letter to her mother written during her first year at Smith College, she notes that she received some words of praise for an essay; her teacher had written on her paper that it was "written with insight and taste and the rare ability to choose the right quotations" (*BU*, 19). The essay, which appears in the May 1925 issue of The *Smith College Monthly,* compares the verse of A. A. Milne and R. L. Stevenson:

> But the verses of Milne tumble informally through the pages. There lies between them and the verses of Stevenson all the difference between the familiar, planned games of children and those original ones that grow up by themselves. Milne's poems express sensations and reactions of children rather than their thoughts and moral feelings. (28)

The observant eye, the fondness for poetry, and the joy in the literature of children that characterize Lindbergh's later work are evident here.

Lindbergh's first story was published in the April 1927 issue of the *Smith College Monthly,* when Lindbergh was in her junior year. Subtitled "A Six O'clock Story for Constance," it is a Lewis Carroll-like story written for Lindbergh's fourteen-year-old younger sister. Also in that issue was an essay entitled "Grand Opera," a review of Edna St. Vincent Millay's text for music composed by Deems Taylor. Lindbergh's creative output continued, as two more prose works were published in the *Smith College Monthly* her senior year; one was a prize-winning essay, "Madame d'Houdetot" (October 1927), and the other a prize-winning story, "'Lida was Beautiful" (June 1928). In addition, Lindbergh saw eight poems published in the college magazine from October 1926 through June 1928; these included "Caprice," "Unicorn," "Letter with a Foreign Stamp," and "Remembrance," reprinted in the *Literary Digest* after her engagement to Charles Lindbergh was announced.

While the world was following the progress of the flight of the man who was to become her husband, Anne Morrow Lindbergh was largely oblivious to the entire event: "When Lindbergh flew the Atlantic, I was buried in the Smith College library writing a paper on Erasmus, in whom I saw a resemblance to my father, a moderate and a peacemaker" (*WW*, xiv). She had begun keeping a diary before she entered Smith College, but her experiences there provided her with subject matter, and she gradually began to develop the practice of making frequent entries. Although the early diary entries are primarily concerned with daily activities, they give ample evidence of her early interest in writing. An edited collection of her diaries and letters was published later, from 1974 to 1980, and they provide helpful infor-

mation about her reactions to the important events in her life. The first
of her published volumes of diaries and letters, *Bring Me a Unicorn*,
chronicles her years at Smith College, her meeting with Charles Lindbergh, and their evolving relationship.

Bring Me a Unicorn

Writing was never something that came easily to Lindbergh, and the
following lament, noted in her diary on 23 October 1927, reappeared,
in different forms, over the next seventeen years:

I want to write—I want to write—I want to write and I never never never
will. I know it and I am so unhappy and it seems as though nothing else
mattered. Whatever I'm doing, it's always there, an ultimate longing there
saying, "Write this—write that—write—" and I *can't*. Lack ability, time,
strength, and duration of vision. I wish someone would tell me brutally, "You
can *never* write *anything*. Take up home gardening!" (*BU*, 82)

Two months after she wrote these thoughts she met Charles Lindbergh.
    After that first meeting she notes in her diary that "this was to be
an objective diary. It stops here!" (88). Even though she was awed by
his presence, she was capable of making an accurate assessment of him:

He is very, very young [Charles was 27; Anne was 21] and was terribly shy—
looked straight ahead and talked in short direct sentences which came out
abruptly and clipped. You could not meet his sentences: they were statements
of fact, presented with such honest directness; not trying to please, just bare
simple answers and statements, not trying to help a conversation along. It
was amazing—breath-taking. I could not speak. What kind of boy was
this? (90)

Attracted to Lindbergh by his sincerity and directness, qualities she
had not often found in other male acquaintances, she thought that he
would prefer the company of her older sister, Elisabeth, who was tall,
blond, and strikingly attractive. But it soon became apparent that
Lindbergh was interested only in Anne. He courted her initially under
the pretense of fulfilling a promise to take her flying, which he did,
several times the following year. By the end of 1928 they were
engaged.
    Lindbergh's appearance in her life gave it a turn she never would
have predicted, for his was a world of machinery, science, action, and

airplanes. Hers had been a world of art, music, and books. But she quickly became caught up in the excitement of the air age that his flight to Paris had ushered in, and she became a staunch proponent of its goals, learning the language and taking flying lessons.

She knew immediately after their meeting, however, that if she were to share his life she would face a difficult challenge in bridging the "chasm" between her interests and his, in accommodating her intellectual goals to a world like his, full of action and technology. After seeing a motion picture entitled *Forty Thousand Miles with Colonel Lindbergh* in Northampton in March 1928, she writes that

> perhaps I could be useful and happy trying to help people to appreciate (by teaching or some other way—writing, *perhaps*) (and perhaps through a family and children) the things I care most about: the beauty and poise and completion of flowers, or birds, of music, of some writing, of some people—glimpses of perfection in all of these. . . . But I cannot dream or hope to do or be anything in that other world. (131)

When she finally confesses to a longtime friend that she will be marrying Lindbergh, she acknowledges that theirs will not be a usual marriage and that usual best wishes will not be appropriate, and she recognizes the difficult challenge ahead—her struggle to achieve artistic self-definition while participating in a life of travel, public attention, and technological activity: "Don't wish me happiness—I don't expect to be happy, but it's gotten beyond that, somehow. Wish me courage and strength and a sense of humor—I will need them all (249)."

Her meeting with Charles Lindbergh changed her mode of life profoundly, a fact graphically illustrated in an accident that befell Charles and Anne shortly before they were married. After their engagement was announced in February 1929, Charles flew down to Mexico City, where Anne was staying with her family at the American embassy. Early in March she and Charles flew from Valbueno Field, in Mexico City, to a nearby prairie, where they enjoyed a quiet picnic lunch together. But when they took off on the return flight to Mexico City, the right wheel on the aircraft fell off. This situation presented a serious problem, for the lack of the wheel meant that the aircraft would almost certainly ground loop (spin around violently) on landing. The resulting maneuver could mean the destruction of the aircraft and personal injury.

Charles, however, was an excellent pilot, and was confident of his ability to manage the aircraft. In preparation for the landing at Mexico City he instructed Anne to place a number of cushions around her and strap in tightly. In landing, the aircraft spun around, and then flipped over on its back. Fortunately, Anne was not hurt, and Charles suffered only a dislocated shoulder. This had been Anne's sixth flight, her fourth with Charles, and their first after the announcement of their engagement. A year earlier, as a senior at Smith College, Anne had been writing essays and reading the poetry of James Elroy Flecker. A year later she was pregnant, earning her glider pilot license, and setting a coast-to-coast flying record with her husband.

Charles Lindbergh and Anne Morrow were married in a private ceremony at the Morrow residence in Englewood, New Jersey, on 27 May, 1929. For their honeymoon they traveled in the Morrows' thirty-eight-foot cabin motorboat, the *Mouette,* from Long Island to Mount Desert Island, Maine, and back. With amazing abruptness Anne Morrow Lindbergh had moved from the quiet world of meditation and books to the raucous world of action and machines.

Chapter Two
Married Life in America

From 1929 through 1935 Lindbergh shared a variety of new experiences with her husband as they flew across the United States on tours promoting air travel as a safe and convenient method of transportation. She gradually settled into the role of her husband's copilot, becoming familiar with aircraft operation and flying procedures. She met hundreds of people in various professions and saw for the first time what the country looked like from the air. Although she was not always completely comfortable with the experience of flying, she determined to fly with her husband and share his adventures firsthand, not to sit at home waiting for his return. The entries in Lindbergh's second volume of diaries and letters, *Hour of Gold, Hour of Lead*, document the challenges she faced.

Hour of Gold, Hour of Lead

Hour of Gold, Hour of Lead is divided into two sharply contrasting parts. The first half, the "hour of gold," describes the first three years of their marriage, from 1929 until the spring of 1932. The major events of this period include their marriage, their flights across the United States, through South America, over North America to the Far East, and the birth of their first child. The second half, the "hour of lead," describes the tragic events of 1932, when their firstborn child was kidnapped and eventually found dead. Although Lindbergh's distress is obvious in her "hour of lead," her "hour of gold" was not without its tribulations.

After the honeymoon the Lindberghs immediately embarked on a series of publicity flights on behalf of the newly inaugurated Transcontinental Air Transport route between New York and Los Angeles. Dubbed the "Lindbergh Line," it was one of the first airlines to begin cross-continent air service, and Charles Lindbergh's presence was instrumental in conveying to the public the safety and convenience of air travel. Anne lent assistance by traveling in the passenger compartment and answering questions put to her by nervous first-time fliers while Charles sat at the controls of the Ford Tri-motor airplane.

In their travels during the summer of 1929 they met many important and unusual people, including Mary Pickford, Amelia Earhart, and President and Mrs. Hoover. In August 1929 they visited the Cleveland Air Races, where Charles flew as a member of a navy demonstration team. In September and October they embarked on a flight into Central and South America at the request of Juan Trippe, president of Pan American Airways. For three weeks in September and October 1929 the Lindberghs accompanied Juan Trippe and his wife Betty on a flying tour of a number of countries in Central and South America. Flying in a twin-engine amphibian, the Sikorsky S-38, the Lindberghs and the Trippes visited Cuba, Haiti, Puerto Rico, Trinidad, Colombia, Venezuela, Panama, Managua, and Belize. Although Charles Lindbergh had flown in the area earlier, in 1927, after he had flown to Mexico City, it was Anne's first flight into the region.

Although Anne discovered that she was pregnant in November, she continued to fly with Charles until shortly before the baby was born. In the spring of 1930 they traveled to California to test-fly their new airplane, the Lockheed Sirius. In January Anne obtained her glider pilot's license, the first woman in the United States to do so. In the first part of April she took instruction in navigation from Harold Gatty, who later flew around the world with Wiley Post. On April 20 the Lindberghs flew from Los Angeles to New York in 14 hours and 45 minutes, setting a new transcontinental speed record; Anne was seven months pregnant at the time.

On 22 June, Anne's birthday, their first child was born. In September 1930 the Lindberghs bought some land near Princeton, New Jersey, where they intended to make their home. Ground was broken for the foundations of their new house in March 1931, and the house was essentially complete by November of that year. The Lindberghs embarked on their flight north across Canada to the Orient in July 1931 and returned in October after learning of the death of Anne's father.

From the summer of 1929 until the summer of 1931, when they departed on their flight across Canada and Alaska to the Far East, they were continually in the public eye. Their life during that two-year period was a continuous series of flights and temporary residences. While this kind of life was initially an interesting change of pace for Anne, it eventually began to take its toll on her creative energies. For, strangely enough, during this two-year period, she never once wrote in her diary; her only written communications consisted of letters to her family members. Lindbergh acknowledged this unusual behavior in the introduction to *Hour of Gold, Hour of Lead,* stating that "the lid of caution" (the result of constant attention from the press and the public) "was clapped down on all spontaneous expression" (*HG,* 6). Her writing output did not decrease during this period, for she faithfully communicated with her usual correspondents—her sisters Elisabeth and Constance, her mother, and Charles's mother, Evangeline Lodge Land Lindbergh. It was not until after the death of her baby that Lindbergh returned to the practice of making diary entries. Two important events mark the beginning and the ending of the "hour of lead"; the first is the kidnapping and death of their first son in March 1932 and the second is the birth of their second son, Jon, in August of that year.

The shock of the kidnapping of Charles, Jr., from their newly built house near Princeton was truly devastating; it was nearly impossible for the Lindberghs to comprehend that someone had climbed into their house through a second-story window in the early evening hours and had taken their sleeping baby while they were going about their family tasks. Although later events strongly indicated that the kidnappers received help from one of the household staff, the fact that the child was taken while they were present in the house troubled them deeply. Although Charles Lindbergh was able to work off many of his anxieties through continuous contact with the law enforcement agencies as they first attempted to recover the child alive and then attempted to apprehend the criminals, Anne had no such outlet. Initially her energy went into communicating with members of the family, both by letter and telephone. But more than communicating with others, she needed to communicate with herself. And so it was, that on 11 May 1932, after a lapse of over three and a half years, she once again began to make diary entries.

The first diary entry, which begins "Woke from a dream of the return of the baby . . ." (247), was dated almost two and a half months after the baby had been taken; the baby's body was found the next day. The diary entries that follow reflect feelings of profound sorrow and dull shock. Lindbergh recalls many of the details of her last days with the baby and, by writing about them, begins the slow process of healing and recovery. But even as she gives voice to her sorrow, she engages in a process of self-definition:

I think . . . women take and conquer sorrow differently from men. They take it willingly, with open arms they blend and merge it into every part of their lives; it is diffused and spread into every fiber, and they build from that and with that. While men take the concentrated bitter dose at one draught and then try to forget—start to work at something objective and entirely separate. [9 June 1932] (270)

This early entry illustrates the essential Lindbergh creative process at work; the diary entry first describes the emotional response to an important personal event. Then a process of analysis begins, as Lindbergh assesses the meaning of the event she has described. Out of this analysis comes insight and the motivation to build upon the experience. In an effort to occupy herself after the baby's death she returned to the task of drafting a first version of *North to the Orient*. But more therapeutic than work on her book was the birth of her second child, who arrived on 16 August.

Her diary entry describing the birth of her baby occupies over four pages of *Hour of Gold* and is clearly of major importance. Because she kept no diary at the time her first child was born, this recollection of the pains and pleasures of birth was a new and special experience, and the arrival of the baby seems to signal a true renewal in her outlook:

I felt as if a great burden had fallen off me. I could not imagine the baby would do this for me, but I felt life given back to me—a door to life opened. I *wanted* to live, I felt power to live. I was not afraid of death or life: a spell had been broken, the spell over us that made me dread everything and feel that nothing would go right after this. The spell was broken by this real, tangible, perfect baby, coming into an imperfect world and coming out of the teeth of sorrow—a miracle. My faith had been reborn. (302)

That the Lindberghs were not fully ready to believe in the miracle of the baby's arrival is indicated in the fact that they were unable to decide on a name for the baby until two months after it was born (320). On 13 September the Lindberghs flew up to the Morrow summer home at North Haven, Maine, for their first visit since their departure for the Orient over a year earlier. As they approached the Penobscot Bay island on which the summer home was located, Lindbergh was able to recapture a sense of joy like that she felt the previous year. As she looks down from the circling aircraft on the small figures of her mother and sister, she is overcome with emotion:

I felt a terrible pity for them and for all of us struggling in this great plan we can't grasp or understand, trying to see when we haven't the power, or the height. If I could only have this height always—but we were coming down now, the pine trees were near and familiar, everyday and human; I was coming down into the world again—the human world. The wind was cold on my face and I had been crying. (315)

This emotional passage of personal response to recent events marks the beginning of the emphasis on the importance of perception, of seeing clearly, with which Lindbergh's works, especially *North to the Orient,* are so intensely occupied.

Locked Rooms and Open Doors

The third volume of Lindbergh's diaries and letters describes the events from 1933 through 1935. The milestones of this three-year span include their flight to Greenland, Europe, and South America, which took place in 1933; completion of *North to the Orient*; and the 1935 Bruno Hauptmann trial. During this three-year period the Lindberghs were essentially homeless, having moved out of their New Jersey home within a year after the kidnapping of their child. When they were not traveling (which they did frequently), they resided in the Morrow household in Englewood, New Jersey, or in the Morrow summer home, in North Haven, Maine. Although the Morrow residences offered the Lindberghs sanctuaries where they could be protected from intrusion by the public, they began to feel themselves trapped in the Morrow environment, and this feeling of restriction adversely affected both Lindberghs. Although Charles could always find an excuse to fly to some part of the country, Anne was not interested in flying to escape; she preferred solitude and quiet. She was more interested in self-discovery and writing. Her diary entries, especially during the latter part of this period, reveal an intense concentration on the determination of her purpose and mode as a writer.

The early diary entries of 1933 are tentative; Lindbergh was still in shock over the death of her first baby, a shock that the arrival of the second baby could not easily assuage. She could not bring herself to begin serious work on the *North to the Orient* manuscript. From July through December they were engaged in their second major flight across large geographical areas of the world, from Maine to Greenland, Scandinavia, Europe, the west coast of Africa, and South America.

Unlike her practice on their first trip, Lindbergh kept copious notes of this flight; while her accounts of the Orient flight occupied only forty pages of *Hour of Gold,* her accounts of the 1933 flight occupy almost 140 pages of *Locked Rooms and Open Doors.*

Lindbergh does not appear to have been as enthusiastic about the 1933 flight as she was in 1931. In the first place, the Lindberghs were traveling for a more extended period of time in remote areas in Greenland; then, when they arrived in Europe, neither one cared for the publicity and crowds that awaited their every stop. Only after they left Portugal and flew to the west coast of Africa did she become more interested in their progress. But by that time they had been traveling in their airplane for nearly five months, and Lindbergh was tired of traveling and was anxious to return to the United States to see her baby. For these reasons, then, her diary entries and letters during this flight are much more about herself and her reactions than about people and places they visit. In Lindbergh's response to watching the native Greenlanders engage in some country dancing, for instance, her interest is centered on herself rather than on the visual details of the dance:

I watch fascinated, and wonder, caught up in the pattern of it, if there is anything more wonderful than this: pattern and design and rhythm.

I had not expected to find it here, though of course it is everywhere, if one is only tuned to it. Flying has it, and life itself, the beat of the heart and the rhythm of respiration. And the pattern of life has it, if I could only realize it. Birth, and love, and death. I try to realize that it would not be complete without death, that death is part of the pattern, and so I must not be afraid of it. (*LR,* 63)

After the flight concluded in December 1933, Lindbergh once again was able to turn her attention to the preparation of her *Orient* manuscript. She was excited by the favorable response the British writer Harold Nicolson gave to her *National Geographic* article, "Flying around the Atlantic," which had been published in September of that year. Nicolson had been spending time in the Morrow household in New Jersey taking notes and gathering information for a biography of Anne's father, Dwight Morrow, which was published the following year. Nicolson's comments provided Lindbergh with the encouragement she needed, and she increasingly validated her commitment to writing: "I can't help taking writing seriously" (15 November 1934) (216).

In December her elder sister, Elisabeth Morrow Morgan, died of heart disease at the age of thirty. The death of her sister was the third in a series of losses of family members that deeply affected Lindbergh. The sadness that she felt at the loss of her sister was compounded by the fact that the trial of Bruno Hauptmann, who had been charged with the murder of the Lindbergh baby, began the first week of January. The pressures of these events and the lack of freedom brought on by the publicity of the trial combined to force Lindbergh into a profoundly unhappy frame of mind:

Sunday, January 20, 1935 . . . I must not talk. I must not cry. I must not write—I most not think—I must not dream. I must control my mind—I must control my body—I must control my emotions—I must finish the book [*North to the Orient*]—I must put up an appearance, at least, of calm for C. I must force myself to be interested in plans, in work, in Jon. I must eat. I must sleep. . . .
    I felt I could understand insanity and physical violence. I could understand anything. (240–41)

Yet she persevered in spite of these frustrations. She continued to work on the revisions to her *Orient* manuscript, pausing briefly to accept an honorary Master of Arts degree from Smith College in June. Lindbergh was overwhelmed with excitement when she learned that Harcourt, Brace & Co. had accepted her book for publication. She was asked to make a few revisions in the manuscript, and the book was published 15 August.

The Lindberghs spent an enjoyable summer of 1935 at the Morrow home at North Haven; they even toyed briefly with the idea of building a home on nearby Matinicus Island. But they returned to the Morrow home in New Jersey at the end of October; by the first of December Charles had grown angry at the invasion of privacy they suffered at the hands of the press, and by 21 December they were sailing for England.

Lindbergh's focus in her diary entries in *Locked Rooms and Open Doors* is much more narrowly directed than in her earlier entries. Even on their 1933 trip she is as much concerned with her own patterns of interpretation of the events she witnesses as she is with the events themselves. Her diary entries are less like a logbook for a lecture series and more like a collection of reference material for future reflection and processing. After their return to the United States she becomes increasingly preoccupied with her potential for writing and her development as a writer. Whereas in *Hour of Gold, Hour of Lead* she appears to be recording the sensations of her new life in a kind of documentary fashion with a husband who was continually on the move, in *Locked Rooms* she is moving to a much more introspective mode of recording her daily activities. In *The Flower and the Nettle* this trend is continued and refined.

Chapter Three
The European Years

In the beginning of 1936 Lindbergh once again was dislocated from an established residence. Although she shared her husband's concerns about the excessive intrusions of the press, she was not completely happy about their sudden move to Europe. However, once they settled into their new home in Long Barn, her sense of comfort, security, and productivity increased significantly. Subsequent travels across Europe, especially in France, helped her to develop a lasting fondness for the peoples and cultures of the Continent.

The Flower and the Nettle

The Flower and the Nettle contains Lindbergh's diary entries and letters from January 1936 through the middle of April, 1939. The volume begins as Lindbergh, her son Jon, and her husband are en route from America to England, and ends as she returns from France to America prior to the onset of World War II. The years Lindbergh spent in Europe were no less event-filled than her years in America; once again she found herself accompanying her husband on his aerial journeys, frequently interrupting the pleasant routine of a settled existence in England and then France to share his experiences. Because they lived in Europe for an extended period of time and found themselves caught up in social and political events in a number of countries, her diary entries are detailed and lengthy; in fact, this volume is the longest of the five, running to some six hundred pages.

The pattern of introspective commentary that was begun in the previous volume is initially interrupted by the sudden change of scene from America to England and by subsequent flights to a number of European countries. But an undercurrent of evaluation is always present and grows in intensity toward the end of the period, when the novelty of the new environment has worn off and the threat of war has grown large. There is an increasing sense of Lindbergh's attempt to reconcile conflicting desires for creative independence and a need to share in her husband's adventures. This tension is never fully resolved, and in fact can be detected even in the title she chose for this volume, which is derived from Shakespeare's *Henry IV*: "Out of this nettle, danger, we have plucked this flower, safety" (*FN*, 419). Although this quotation is linked specifically to Chamberlain's attempt to appease Hitler in September 1938, it also refers to the Lindbergh family experiences in general, and to Anne Lindbergh's competing urges to participate in her husband's activities and to devote more time to her writing.

The most important event in 1936 was their move into Long Barn, the English country residence of Harold Nicolson and his wife, Vita Sackville-West. This residence, in a secluded and gardenlike location, gave Lindbergh the privacy and the aesthetic pleasure for which she had been searching; in addition to providing an ideal location in which her son could play, it also gave her the kind of surroundings she needed to finish working on her second book, *Listen! the Wind*. An early 1936 diary entry indicates her delight with their new domicile: "It was evening and very peaceful and C. and I laughed—for joy, really, such a house! I had an incredible feeling of peace and security—the low house backed up to a hill, its arms around you. . . . I found myself laughing and laughing, for joy and relief and amusement at the place" (25).

Lindbergh is initially reluctant to travel with her husband; her reaction is understandable, for no sooner has she unpacked in their new home (in March 1936) than he intends to travel to France. She is torn by her desire to write and her desire to travel with him: "Who am I to say No, I want my own life, No, I want my own work, No, I will not go to Africa because I want to finish a book. Of what value would that book be? A personal account of hashed-over dead experiences. Of what value, next to the vision, the new ways that C. can give, and I by keeping him happy, by doing what he wants?" (44). Her conflicting urges about accompanying her husband were further complicated by the fact that their presence was increasingly desired by numerous socially and politically important people, including Lord and Lady Astor, Ambassador Kennedy, even King Edward VIII and Mrs. Simpson. In July they flew to Germany for the first of three visits, where they met Hermann Goering, Erhardt Milch, and Ernst Udet, all key figures involved in the development of German aviation. As the year ended she discovered that she was going to have another child.

The first major activity of 1937 was a flight to Italy and India in

February and March; the first portion of this flight, from England to Italy, was used as the basis for *The Steep Ascent*. They returned to England in time for the coronation of George VI, who was crowned after Edward abdicated. But the birth of the third child, Land, prevented their attendance at the coronation. In October they flew to Germany for the second time that year, and in November they sailed for America to spend Christmas at the Morrow residence in New Jersey. They returned to England in March. Their two children were left in the care of a governess at Long Barn during the four months they were in America.

After their return in March they were primarily occupied with a move to Illiec, a small island off the coast of France. Charles wanted to move there because he could be closer to Alexis Carrel and his wife; he had been working intensively with Carrel, a doctor who specialized in heart surgery, on the development of an early version of a heart pump. Anne was not fully happy about leaving Long Barn, but the idea of Illiec was not without its appeal, primarily because it reminded her of the Morrow summer home in North Haven. Her social life was filled with activity in the month before they moved to Illiec, for Lady Astor invited them to a luncheon for George Bernard Shaw on the fifth of May at which Ambassador to France William Bullitt and Ambassador to England Joseph P. Kennedy were also in attendance. Just over two weeks later they attended a ball given by the Astors where they met the Duke and Duchess of Kent, Viscount and Viscountess Cranbourne, and the newly crowned King George VI and Queen Elizabeth.

Lindbergh spent most of June and July installing the family and establishing some order in their house in Illiec; she also managed to polish the *Listen! the Wind* manuscript in June and review the proofs that Harcourt, Brace sent her in July. By the first week of August she was once again flying with her husband, this time to Russia, where he was conferring with military and civilian aviation specialists. They were away on this trip until the middle of September. By the end of September they were back in London, visiting the Astors, and nervously awaiting the resolution of the Munich crisis. During this time Lindbergh was actively involved in numerous discussions with the Astors and others about the prospect and need for world peace. Many of the arguments that she included in her "Prayer for Peace" and *The Wave of the Future* were first formulated during their visits with the Astors in 1938.

The Lindberghs returned to Illiec on the first of October, and by the ninth were once again en route to Germany, where Charles had been invited for another visit with German aviation officials. It was during this visit, on 18 October, that Hermann Goering unexpectedly presented Charles Lindbergh with a civilian aviation achievement medal. This incident was used later by critics to suggest that Lindbergh was favorably inclined toward the Germans. While Lindbergh certainly was impressed with their aviation technology and political efficiency, he never gave his support to any German cause, then or later.

They were back in Illiec by the first of November and decided to relocate to Paris for the winter. They found an apartment by the twenty-fourth in which they lived until they left for America the following April. In the four months in which they lived in Paris they returned twice to visit the Astors in London, once at the end of January and once at the end of February. Their social life was an active one in Paris; they entertained occasionally in their apartment and were invited to a number of diplomatic affairs. One of the more memorable occurred on 7 February, when they attended a dinner hosted at the American embassy where they talked to a number of distinguished cultural and diplomatic guests, including the Duke and Duchess of Windsor, Minister for Air Guy La Chambre and his wife, the Duc and Duchesse de La Rochefoucauld, the wife of André Maurois, Ambassador Kennedy, and Ambassador Bullitt (501–12).

Prior to Lindbergh's departure for the United States, she began re-reading her diaries that she had kept ten years earlier. She is struck by her youthful idealism and the impact of her encounter with Charles:

I can see how there was a long inarticulate period in my life because (so like the young), in my admiration for him and his world, I tossed aside my own as worth nothing and I struggled to lose myself in his, which was after all Life itself. I was plunged into life—active life—loving and living and having children and those terrific trips and the suffering too.

But now it is coming into its own again, that early world of writing and thinking, stronger and realer and richer, and impregnated with C. and with his life and what he has taught me.

And there is no longer that terrific struggle between the two—that divided self—that was there for years. That old self, suppressed, passionate, insisting to come out—pushed down by that other new self, practical, active, outward, and comparatively efficient.

No; somehow they have fused—at least I think so. At last they are one. (518)

Although Lindbergh's conclusion is tentative, she feels that she has been able to accommodate with some success the roles of writer and companion to her husband. The split in her two worlds that begins in *Hour of Gold, Hour of Lead* and reaches its most extreme condition in *Locked Rooms and Open Doors* is nearly mended in *The Flower and the Nettle.* In the last of her five volumes of diaries and letters, *War Within and Without,* she finds the outlook and the voice that can best express her vision of artistic wholeness.

War Within and Without

The final volume of Lindbergh's diaries and letters has, like its predecessors, its own structural unity, defined in this instance by the conditions of Lindbergh's association with the French writer and aviator, Antoine de Saint-Exupéry. She met him shortly after she returned to the United States from France, in the late summer of 1939, when he visited the Lindberghs in their Long Island home. The period ended with his death while he was flying a military reconnaissance mission in July 1944; her last recorded diary entry, on 27 October 1944, is partially a remembrance of him. Lindbergh thought of him frequently during this five-year period, and she worked intently to incorporate his philosophic mode of spiritual significance in her writings. His voice serves as an artistic conscience by which she measured her own achievements.

After the Lindberghs returned to the United States in April 1939, they once again established their pattern of moving from one residence to another, as they attempted to determine their own best course of action. For a brief period Charles worked with the Army Air Force personnel, in the summer of 1939, and then, after the war began in Europe, he lent his voice to the isolationist cause during most of 1940 and 1941. Anne followed her husband, managed the family, and developed her own peace-oriented perspective on the war.

Their first residence was on Lloyd Neck, Long Island; they moved in on 23 June, the day after Anne's birthday, and remained there until August 1941. Anne was pleased with the location because it offered a view of Long Island Sound and provided a safe environment for her two young children. The most memorable event of their stay there, however, occurred only six weeks after they moved in: Antoine de Saint-Exupéry stayed with them for two nights, on the fifth and sixth of August.

Saint-Exupéry had come to America in connection with the publication of *Wind, Sand and Stars*; before he left France he had been given a copy of Lindbergh's *Listen! the Wind* and had been asked to write a preface for the French edition. He was favorably impressed with the book and upon arriving indicated a desire to meet Lindbergh. From the moment they met in New York City, where she went to bring him out to her Long Island home, they engaged in a nonstop conversation on writing, writers, and flying. When Charles arrived, the discussion continued, Anne translating from French to English for her husband's benefit. Saint-Exupéry's whirlwind visit made a deep impression on Lindbergh; she was totally enthralled by his alertness and depth: "My mind has been quickened, and my sight and feelings. For a week now the world has been almost unbearably beautiful. . . . It is too much" (*WW*, 35). Less than three weeks later Saint-Exupéry sailed back to France, worried about the German crisis.

Moved to return the compliment Saint-Exupéry had paid her in his preface to the French edition of *Listen! the Wind*, Lindbergh immediately began to draft a review of *Wind, Sand and Stars*. The review was published in the 14 October 1939 issue of the *Saturday Review* and was added to the eighth edition of *Wind, Sand and Stars* as a preface; later editions, however, omitted it after the Lindberghs became unfavorably identified with the isolationist movement (*WW*, 250–51). In her review Lindbergh addresses the same issue that Saint-Exupéry had discussed in his preface to her book, that flatly factual reporting of events is less successful and less important than an informed interpretation of those events.

Bolstered by Saint-Exupéry's remarks, Lindbergh argues that events are best assessed after the passage of time and personal reflection. She interprets Saint-Exupéry's writing as the heightening of experience and of expanding human perception. She describes this process as a challenge to the writer to become participant and observer simultaneously, to become both "the actor and the onlooker" (9). In accounting for the special qualities of Saint-Exupéry's writing, Lindbergh provides an account of her own compositional approach. She recalls a response she once gave to a friend who had asked her if she had thought the exact thoughts she had described in one of her books while she was actually engaged in flying:

If I did not have exactly those words and thoughts, I had at least a sensation. I had an emotion; and I gathered that seed. I plucked off the hour hastily, in passing, without cracking it open. I took it home with me, not knowing when that pod would deliver its secret to me, but hoping that some day it would, if only I were patient. (For one must not pry it open. One must never force the secret out. That would be dishonest and sentimental.) Sometimes one waits years for these strange inner harvests, these "emotions recollected in tranquility." . . .

No, I feel, it is not sentimentalizing to attribute your present thoughts to past action—even though on first glance it seems to be. (9)

This passage effectively summarizes Lindbergh's compositional method, and her reference to Wordsworth indicates her kinship with the romantic tradition.

From the time the Germans invaded Poland until the Japanese attack on Pearl Harbor, Charles Lindbergh was involved in a campaign to prevent what he saw as a dangerous tendency in America to enter a war it was ill prepared to fight. To this end he delivered twelve addresses to the American public, over the radio or in person. During this period Anne was attempting to formulate her opposition to the war. Although she shared her husband's fear of precipitous American participation, her objection was based on a philosophical ideal, while his grew out of technical knowledge. He felt America lacked equipment and know-how; she felt America lacked the appropriate philosophical perspective. As she explained in a letter to her mother, written 5 June 1940, her view "is not as strictly pacifist a view as it sounds. It is the conclusion in part I have come to, the bridge I have been forced to build between C's logic and factual judgment and my own philosophy or religion" (100).

Because her mother was lending moral and financial assistance to causes that did not agree with the Lindberghs' views, this was a particularly difficult time. The discomfort that developed during the summer of 1940 was derived from a number of causes. The most obvious was the tension resulting from attacks against their isolationist stand that were appearing in the press and in the occasional threatening letters they received in the mail. Additional tension resulted from internal disagreement in the Morrow family regarding American involvement. Lindbergh increasingly turned to writing in her diary as a way of articulating and recognizing her doubts and fears. Her diary entries, especially in 1940 and 1941, are among her most intellectually troubled and emotionally revealing.

The pressure and the uncertainty of the war caused Lindbergh and her husband to engage in a number of discussions about the progress of their work and their long-range goals. One such discussion, which occurred toward the end of July 1940, illustrates Lindbergh's frustrations. She writes that Charles had been discussing the progress of her writing: "he goes over the record—nine years, and only two books and wonders why it is. Has he not given me the right kind of environment?" (129). She acknowledges that she is too easily distracted by other tasks because she feels the burden of the writing she should be doing:

But you ask too much, I want to cry out. I cannot be having a baby and be a good housekeeper and keep thinking and writing on the present times (in my diary) and be always free to discuss anything with you and give to the children and keep an atmosphere of peace in the family (the bigger family which is so scattered and distraught now, all of us disagreeing) and keep my mind clear and open on the present-day things and write a book at the same time. (130)

And then, as she is effectively describing her frustrations to herself, she is caught up in the progress of her own thought. What is the "permanent writing" she should be doing? Not the kind of writing she was doing before the war, she decides; the war has closed that route, practically and philosophically.

I have the feeling I must begin again, as one has to begin life again now, with an utterly new conception, new ideals, new words even. But we are just learning them. The new age is just beginning. In fact, it is the transition stage. The old world is dying and a new one beginning, and this is the pain and uncertainty and anguish we all feel. How can I write in the new language before that world is born? (130–31)

This remarkable sequence illustrates the manner in which the materials that contribute to personal tension are transmuted into artistic insight and eventually into finished creative work. The "new language" of the world that will be born of the war, for instance, began to be articulated in *The Wave of the Future,* the brief but controversial work that Lindbergh completed the following month.

Charles Lindbergh encouraged his wife to devote increased attention to her writing and to this end arranged to have her diaries consolidated and typed. Anne Lindbergh was initially not certain that this was a good idea, and the entire project forced her to evaluate the purpose and value that her diaries possess. Dismayed at their youthful naïveté, she at first questions the merit of such an undertaking, but eventually decides that it is absolutely essential that she write them:

And *now*, am I writing what at fifty I shall think trash? No matter, one has to write, one writes not to be read but to breathe—I did even then. One writes to think, to pray, to analyze. One writes to clear one's mind, to dissipate one's fears, to face one's doubts, to look at one's mistakes—in order to retrieve them. One writes to capture and crystallize one's joy, but also to analyze and disperse one's gloom. (167)

In August 1941 the Lindberghs moved again, this time to Seven Gates Farm, on Martha's Vineyard. They continued their noninterventionist activities for a time, abandoning those activities after the attack on Pearl Harbor. Charles volunteered his services to the government, but was refused. He found work with Henry Ford as a civilian test pilot at the Ford plant near Dearborn, Michigan. Ford had long been an admirer of Lindbergh's technical knowledge, and Ford, like Lindbergh, had been an ardent noninterventionist. Lindbergh flew aircraft that were being built at the Ford plant, specializing particularly in high-altitude and long-range test flights. Anne and the family eventually joined Charles in June 1942, when they rented a house in Bloomfield Hills. The Lindberghs maintained this residence until September 1944. Two months after her arrival in Detroit, Anne Lindbergh gave birth to her fifth child and third boy, Scott. Anne, their first daughter, had been born in October 1940, while they were living at Lloyd Neck.

Lindbergh's primary creative activity during her stay in Detroit was *The Steep Ascent*, which she was engaged in writing from December 1942 until November 1943. But equal in importance to her published work is her attention to her diary. As her husband became increasingly involved in his test-flying work, he was once again absent from the house, and Lindbergh turned to her diary to gain a sense of balance and purpose.

Why is it so vital to do so? What justification have I in writing in my diary when I might be heaping up pages of a book, as C. is doing *in his spare time* [on *The Spirit of St. Louis*]. . . . And yet my life does not go well *without* writing. It is my flywheel, my cloister, my communication with myself and God. It is my eyes to the world, my window for awareness, without which I cannot see anything or walk straight. Writing in a diary is my tool for the development of awareness. It is the crucible through which the rough material of life must pass before I can use it in art. (360)

The concluding period described in Lindbergh's final volume of diaries and letters extends from April through October of 1944. In April Charles left for the Pacific theater of operations, where he was involved in test-flying the P-38, primarily in demonstrating long-range cruise-control characteristics to the combat pilots of the area who were required to fly long distances across the Pacific Ocean. In his absence Anne Lindbergh was plunged into an emotional and creative limbo, during which she wrote nothing of note, even avoiding making any diary entries. Only when her husband returned in October 1944 did she resume recording her thoughts in her diary. This lack of creative energy confirmed what she had acknowledged earlier, that her creative activity was nourished by her nearness to her husband, even though that nearness often brought a significant increase in traveling and other physical activities.

But this period was not an unproductive period in Lindbergh's life, for, forced to leave Detroit when the lease on their rented house expired, she traveled to Connecticut, found a new residence for the family, and moved her four children and all of their personal belongings into the residence prior to her husband's return from the Pacific. The closing chapter of her published volumes of diaries and letters concludes with her acknowledgment that three important events had all occurred within days of one another: one was her husband's return; the second was the liberation of Paris, which signified the freeing of that part of Europe that she most closely identified with; and the third was the news of the death of Saint-Exupéry, the man who had made such a deep impression on her, emotionally as well as intellectually (440–52).

The Value of the Diaries and Letters

Lindbergh's published diaries and letters may well prove to be the most enduring of her written works. They reveal the creative processes of a talented and perceptive writer; they provide an insight into the life of her husband, one of the most unusual and controversial fliers of the twentieth century; they describe numerous important historical events; they contain accurate portraits of several major personages of the period; and they chronicle twenty-five of the most important years of the century. The woman who wrote these diary entries and letters was struggling to give shape to the events and ideas that surrounded her. They were, as Lindbergh herself acknowledged, a "crucible" through which she passed the daily experiences of her life in order to determine as best she could their meaning and impact. The appeal of these volumes is in their repeated verbal assessment, in the changes that occur as the ideas and opinions are constantly reviewed and examined. Because Lindbergh is constantly questioning her responses and her motives, these writings reflect the vitality of her continuous process of self-definition.

Chapter Four
North to the Orient

In *North to the Orient* Lindbergh recaptures the sensations of excitement and awe that she felt when she and her husband embarked on their 1931 flight to Canada, Alaska, and the Orient. The book conveys the newness of the experience and describes her development from apprentice to seasoned crew member. At a deeper level, however, the book addresses the theme of *perception*. Throughout the narrative Lindbergh consistently attempts to ensure that she is observing the scenes of the journey accurately and that she understands their full meaning; the primary thematic focus of the book is the sharpening and clarifying of powers of seeing. As the flight progresses, every event and every object becomes increasingly important in developing an awareness of the peoples and experiences of the world and of the meanings they possess. The emphasis on perception in the book is first established at the departure from North Haven and concludes with the discovery of the "most beautiful pagoda" in the interior of China.

In the spring of 1931 the Lindberghs prepared for their first major aerial survey flight across Canada and Alaska to the Orient. It was intended to obtain information for Juan Terry Trippe's Pan American Airways to determine the feasibility of routing commercial air transportation flights across the polar areas. Improvements in aircraft range and payload were making longer flights increasingly feasible, and visionaries like Trippe knew that the shortest intercontinental routes would lie across northern areas. In preparation for this flight Anne undertook two significant tasks: she obtained her pilot's license and she learned to operate a high-frequency radio set and to transmit and receive Morse code. Both accomplishments were necessary for the success of the flight.

The flight north to the Orient began on 27 July 1931, when the Lindberghs left Flushing Bay, Long Island, New York, and it ended on 2 October in the waters of the Yangtze River in China. The route they followed during the two-and-a-half month trip took them to Washington, D.C., and then to North Haven, Maine, where they said good-bye to the Morrow family at their summer residence. After departing North Haven, they flew directly to Ottawa, Ontario, and then to Churchill, Manitoba; Baker Lake and Aklavik, both in the Northwest Territories; Point Barrow and Nome, Alaska; the Kamchatka Peninsula, in Russian territory; Tokyo and Osaka, Japan; and Nanking, China. Their journey ended unexpectedly when their aircraft was tipped into the Yangtze River. The Lindberghs had originally planned to continue their journey around the world, but the water damage to their aircraft and the news of her father's death caused them to change their plans and return to the United States.

Preparation of the Manuscript

Although she began work on the manuscript that was to become *North to the Orient* immediately after their return to the United States, a number of events prevented her from completing the work for four years. The first of these was the kidnapping and murder of their firstborn boy in March 1932; the second event was their second extended aerial survey trip, which took place from July to December 1933. The last interruption was the trial of Bruno Hauptmann, who had been charged with the death of her child, in January and February 1935.

The distress of the kidnapping upset Lindbergh's creative efforts for nearly four months. The repercussions of the deaths of her father and firstborn child affected her efforts to unify the manuscript. As early as 26 June 1932, three months after the kidnapping, she notes in her diary her difficulty in seeing its wholeness: "I do not see it whole with a single clear idea in it. There is no design—it is just narrative" (*HG,* 283).

The primary challenge that she faced in the preparation of the book was the magnitude of the trip; they had been gone for nearly seventy days, had made over twenty-five stops, and had met hundreds of people. In addition, she was faced with the substantial problem of trying to recapture the spirit of excitement and enthusiasm she had felt during the trip, a problem compounded by the fact that she had kept no diary entries during the trip. She had essentially stopped writing in her diary from the time of her wedding until two months after the kidnapping of the baby. Her only reference materials for the preparation of the manuscript were the letters she had written to her mother, primarily, although she had also written to her sister Elisabeth and to Mrs. Lindbergh. These letters were subsequently published in the second volume of her diaries and letters, *Hour of Gold, Hour of Lead* (164–202). She borrowed from these letters when she put together the *Orient* manuscript, for many passages in the book resemble those in the letters. But many of the descriptive sections in the book were written later, long after the flight had concluded. Of the twenty-three chapters in the book, fifteen are drawn more or less directly from passages first recorded in her letters home. Eight of the chapters and the preface consist primarily of material added later. And of the fifteen chapters based on material in her letters, six contain long sections added later.

Lindbergh worked steadily, if slowly, on the *Orient* manuscript for the first six months of 1933, and then had to set it aside as she and Charles embarked on their second flight, this one to Greenland, Europe, Africa, and South America, which occupied them from July through December. The most intense and extended period of writing occurred from January 1934 to January 1935. A first draft of *North to the Orient* was completed in early June 1934, but revisions were delayed for two months while Lindbergh completed work on a *National Geographic* article ("Flying Around the Atlantic") that she had promised to deliver (*LR*, 192–95). Evidently the first draft of the *Orient* manuscript consisted of reworkings of her letters home, for her diary entries after June 1934 indicate that she was reading other materials in preparation for portions of the manuscript added later. An entry of 23 August notes that she has been reading excerpts from Hakluyt's *Voyages* (196); an extended reference to Hakluyt appears in chapter 1.

In a letter to her sister Elisabeth written mid-October 1934 Lindbergh comments that she has just written "two new chapters—one, a preface, and one an introduction" (*LR*, 204), and it seems clear that she was incorporating the Hakluyt material at this time. She was still having difficulty finding a unifying pattern, a thematic focus:

The book is already in two badly glued sections: One—humorous, slightly slapstick, setting-out-to-be-a *Geographic* article (about five chapters). Two— more serious, more pointed-up, more or less "theme" chapters (about seventeen). Then my new beginning—still more serious and vague and pseudo-philosophical than the "theme" chapters. Everything new I write throws the rest out of kilter. It is just like a room decorated at different periods. (*LR*, 204–5)

Compounding her unhappiness, in December her sister Elisabeth died, and in January the Lindberghs were forced to relive the days of the kidnapping of their baby, for Bruno Hauptmann, who had been arrested in September, went to trial the first week of January. Nevertheless, Lindbergh continued to work at the manuscript during the winter months. She noted in her diary for 5 March that she was still "correcting" some chapters (*LR*, 257). By the end of April it was in the hands of Harcourt, Brace; it was published in August.

Vision and Theme

The problem Lindbergh faced in shaping the material that constituted *North to the Orient* was establishing a unity of vision. Because she had gotten out of the habit of writing in her diary, her primary record of the flight consisted of her letters home. She also imposed a self-censoring mechanism in her letters that prevented a complete picture of their adventures. She described this situation later in life, in her preface to *Hour of Gold, Hour of Lead*:

Travel impressions they were on the whole, and somewhat played down. My inner censor was at work, keeping a strict watch on what I wrote. And my protective instinct about my family made me hold back on the more hazardous episodes. The intention of the letters was partly to reassure. I touched rather lightly on the dangers until we arrived safely home. (*HG*, 10–11)

Lindbergh resolved the dilemma by directly confronting the essential problem, by directing the focal thematic point of the book toward the idea of her own interpretive perception of the major events she experienced on the trip. The result of this emphasis on perception is a narrative that begins as a casual, nonselective collection of visual images but that moves gradually toward a sequence of more limited images that possess more complex meanings. This approach was at least partly the result of Lindbergh's attempt to recapture her mood at a happier time in her life, when all of her family members were still alive; the attempt to recapture that mood involved the effort to "resee" in her mind the events of that period.

The preface of *North to the Orient* outlines Lindbergh's method. She suggests that her purpose in writing has been partly to recapture her experiences, but primarily to discover their meaning. For "paradoxically," she says, "the more unreal an experience becomes—translated from real action into unreal words, dead symbols for life itself—the more vivid it grows. Not only does it seem more vivid, but its essential core becomes clearer" (NO, 9).

Lindbergh states that the "essential quality" of her narrative is derived from a combination of the flying experience, the places visited, and the time of the flight. The essential quality is like "magic" because the phenomenal technological achievement represented by their aircraft brings them into contact with peoples and communities far removed from modern life. The magic of their flight has presented her with large contrasts between the new and the old methods, between modern civilizations and older cultures, and between isolation and accessibility. The attempt to appreciate these contrasts and the effort to understand their meanings constitute the heart of the book.

The first chapter ("North to the Orient") continues to develop the ideas expressed in the preface. It first establishes a link with, and a contrast to, the Elizabethan explorers, Cabot, Frobisher, Davis, Willoughby. The link is established in a passage she finds of Master George Best in Hakluyt's *Voyages*: "How dangerous it is to attempt new Discoveries . . ." (21). But, as Best continues to comment, travel also offers its rewards, including the discovery of new forms of wildlife, never-before-seen natural wonders, different cultures and forms of government, and treasures material and spiritual. Lindbergh writes: "Travelers are always discoverers, especially those who travel by air. There are no signposts in the sky to show a man has passed that way before. There are no channels marked. The flier breaks each second into new uncharted seas" (22). The connection with the narratives of Hakluyt's *Voyages* is instructive, for it places the work in the tradition of the travel narrative, and it links it to one of the undisputed masterworks of the genre. It is also appropriate because *North to the Orient* is the first of its kind to demonstrate a sense of its own significance as a unique contribution to the modern offshoot of the travel narrative—the aerial travel narrative. Although other aerial travel narratives had appeared prior to World War II, they were, for the most part, dryly factual accounts of the flight experiences and seldom displayed any awareness of the more profound implications of their achievements.

In the conclusion of the opening chapter Lindbergh provides the key to the importance of perception in her account of their travels: "One looks terrified for a visible sign of piercing with the light of human eye the darkness of a hitherto unseen world" (22). Lindbergh becomes increasingly concerned to discover each locale's "visible sign" as they travel along their route, and her account becomes increasingly focused on more and more limited but instructive aspects of the scenes they witness. Whereas the "terror" to which she refers certainly includes some of the more hazardous experiences of the trip, it indicates primarily the intensity of her search for personal meaning in the events of the journey.

Departing the United States

Chapters 2 through 5 describe the Lindberghs' attempt to prepare themselves for their journey and the preliminary flights prior to departing the United States. Chapter 2 ("Preparation") gives a factual account of the many planning decisions that they had to make in advance of their departure: the route, fuel, food, emergency equipment, clothes, and—one of the crucial requirements—the ability to communicate by radio. Lindbergh's account of her struggle to master the intricacies of radio transmission establishes one of the important thematic aspects of the book—her ability to communicate the information that the flight will provide.

In the fourth chapter, "North Haven," Lindbergh begins to settle in to her new environment as crew member and observer of new and unusual sights. The chapter describes her new airborne perspective of a community she knew well previously, but from an earthbound viewpoint. As they depart the Morrow summer home on North Haven Island, Maine, for the next leg of their flight to Ottawa, Canada, Lindbergh sees the island from the air in a special way:

The day was hard and clear and bright, like the light slanting off a white farmhouse. The island falling away under us as we rose in the air lay still and perfect, cut out in starched clarity against a dark sea. I had the keenest satisfaction in embracing it all with my eye. It was mine as though I held it, an apple in my hand. (52)

The meaning of this vision is especially significant because this moment represented the last gathering of the family as she had known it in her youth. Her concluding passage in the chapter captures the essence of her mixed perspective of past and present as she reviews the events of the summer from a vantage point in time several years later:

I had great pleasure in straightening these confusions in my mind, in clarifying the complexities of my childhood world. And this sense of detachment

in space gave me also a sense of detachment in time, as though I were looking
back at my own life from some high point in the future. . . . (53)

The episode is clearly linked to Lindbergh's emotional return to North
Haven in 1932 (*HG*, 315). The circularity of the vision encapsulates
both the fragmentation and the unity of Lindbergh's attempt to put
the events of the flight into a coherent perspective. It is only when the
Lindberghs depart the Morrow summer home on North Haven that
events begin to establish themselves in a meaningful pattern, in which
past episodes signal future events, and present narrative passages recall
the past.

Across Canada and Alaska

The departure from North Haven marked the beginning of the truly
exploratory portion of the flight. Chapter 5 ("Radio and Routes") describes the first of the serious tests they faced in cross-country navigation and communication. The primary challenge that Lindbergh faced
on the flight to Ottawa was her effort to establish radio communications with ground stations en route. Although she initially transcribed
her messages awkwardly and slowly, she successfully transmitted and
received her position and weather reports. To add to her difficulty, she
found that she had continually to retune the station with which she
was communicating, as the movement of the airplane and weather conditions combined to make clear radio reception difficult. Gradually,
after days of sending and receiving Morse code, she found that she
could hear the messages as if she were listening to a normal
conversation.

Lindbergh's efforts to communicate were not limited to mental agil-
ity only; she also expended physical energy in extending the radio antenna. Antenna extension could be accomplished only by turning a
handcrank in her cabin compartment. She had to crank the handle
approximately fifty times to unwind the antenna from the aircraft fuselage, and crank it another fifty turns to wind the antenna back into
the aircraft. It was much more difficult to wind the antenna in than
out because the speed of the aircraft combined with the weight of the
antenna wire to create additional resistance. The antenna had to be
rewound whenever the aircraft descended for landing or flew close to
the terrain, for contact with the ground could snap off the antenna.

In chapter 6 ("Baker Lake") Lindbergh introduces the first in the series of contrasts. As they land on the calm surface of Baker Lake, she notices a sign on a small white shack that says "Revillon Frères Ltd. Furs," and she is immediately reminded of a Fifth Avenue store in Manhattan where Revillon Frères Furs are sold. The juxtaposition of the sophistication of the Fifth Avenue shop and the wilds of northern Canada is the first of many adjustments to usual perception that she will experience. The next, and more pervasive, contrast occurs when she meets the few white male inhabitants of the lonely outpost who refer to the rest of the world as "outside": "What's it like *outside?*" she is asked (68). The implied contrast of freedom versus confinement suggests the notion that life in this remote outpost is in some ways like life in a prison. Lindbergh discovers that her expectations and the truths of her traveling experiences are often not in harmony.

In her attempt to converse with the handful of men who are desperate for some kind of link to the outside world, she discovers the power of the "magic word":

> But to mention a loved object, a person, or a place to someone else is to invest that object with reality. You say the magic word: the listener smiles, an image forming in his thoughts, and then, as though his image were superimposed upon yours, a picture rises out of the dark sea of memory—not the flat photograph which has hung so long on the walls of his mind that it has lost meaning, but a new picture with depth and life and solidity, as though seen through a stereoscope. (71–72)

The "magic word," as Lindbergh characterizes it, enables the speaker and the listener to share a vision that possesses a special significance; the ability to choose the "magic word" encompasses powers of both communication and perception. The "magic word" becomes increasingly important to Lindbergh to visualize the locales and peoples she visits and to describe their distinguishing features.

"Point Barrow" (chapter 8) describes Lindbergh's experiences at the northernmost point of their travels. "Point Barrow" represents the point of farthest reach thematically as well as geographically, for in "Point Barrow" Lindbergh encounters her most important challenge as a communicator, in radio communications efforts over vast distances. She also witnesses the success of the "magic word" as used by the camp doctor, who translates the language of the Bible into metaphors that will have meaning for native people living in an environment of tundra, snow, and ice (105–08).

Up to this point, the chapters of *North to the Orient* closely parallel scenes and events described in Lindbergh's letters home. However, in the next chapter, chapter 9 ("Dark"), she deviates from this pattern; a one-page passage in *Hour of Gold, Hour of Lead* is expanded into an eleven-page chapter. This frequently anthologized chapter describes Lindbergh's fear and anxiety as she and her husband attempt to fly from Point Barrow to Nome. Having become accustomed to continuous sunlight at the latitude of the Arctic Circle, they find themselves losing daylight as they fly south toward Nome. Fog over the mountain range north of Nome causes them to land for the night on an isolated coastline of the Seward Peninsula.

Lindbergh's account of the flight is, in effect, an exploration of the metaphorical meaning of the word *dark*, especially as its meaning pertains to fliers: "Dark—that curfew hour in a flier's mind, when the gates are closed, the portcullis dropped down, and there is no way to go around or to squeeze under the bars if one is late" (113). Lindbergh describes a contrast in their flying conditions that intrigues her, for as they flew north, into colder, more inhospitable country, they found more light, so that they could fly at night as well as day. As they turn south, however, heading back into warmer, more hospitable country, they lose the helpful light and once again experience the unique blindness of night flying. Traveling into the lighted North she describes as "like stepping very quietly across the invisible border of the land of Faery that the Irish poets write of" (113–14), but as they fly into the approaching night, Lindbergh feels "the terror of a savage seeing a first eclipse, or even as if I had never known night" (115).

Across the Pacific to the Orient

Chapter 11 ("Kamchatka") provides another example of Lindbergh's efforts to find the true perspective on the locale she is visiting, in this case two communities on the Russian Kamchatka Peninsula, Karaginski and Petropavlovsk. The chapter opens with a list of the reactions Lindbergh feels she has been conditioned to expect when she encounters the Russian people and political system. But she actually finds a much different experience than that she had been led to believe, at least in Karaginski, where the local villagers and trappers are so much like the natives of Point Barrow and Aklavik that she feels very much at home. She feels especially close to a woman with whom she shares a picture of her young son.

In Petropavlovsk, however, her feeling is different, for that community appears to be much more like the systematic, if disorganized, society she has been led to expect. She concludes the chapter by commenting that although she has seen the experimental farms, schools, and new construction projects, she prefers to recall the brief moments of human contact that she was able to share.

Chapter 12 ("Fog—and the Chishima") returns to the pattern of reconstruction, which began with "Dark," of writing extensive material to supplement initially brief descriptive passages in her letters home. The additional material in this chapter focuses on Lindbergh's emotional reaction to the emergency landing they made near Ketoi Island after they became enveloped in an encroaching fog bank. In this instance they encountered a thick, far-reaching fog bank as they flew over the northern island chain of Japan and were forced to descend in near-zero visibility conditions down the side of a volcanic mountain to attempt a landing in the open sea. The episode begins as Charles girds himself for battle with the elements:

My husband pushed back the cockpit cover, put on his helmet and goggles, heightened the seat for better visibility, and leaned forward to look out. Here we are again, I thought, recognizing by this familiar buckling-on-of-armor that the fight had begun. (153)

Lindbergh's account of their first descent down the mountainside is more emotional, visceral description than visual:

Down, down—the sky was gone. The sea! Hold on to the sea—that little patch of blue. Oh, the sea was gone too. We were blind—and still going down—oh, God!—we'll hit the mountain! A wave of fear like terrific pain swept over me, shriveling to blackened ashes the meaningless words "courage"—"pride"—"control." Then a lurch, the engine roared on again, and a sickening roller-coaster up. Up, up, up. I felt myself gasping to get up, like a drowning man. There—the sky was blue above—the sky and the sun! Courage flowed back in my veins, a warm, pounding stream. Thank God, there is the sky. Hold on to it with both hands. Let it pull you up. Oh, let us stay here, I thought, up in this clear bright world of reality, where we can see the sky and feel the sun. Let's never go down. (155)

This episode vividly illustrates an aspect of the learning process associated with their journey that has become increasingly evident—they are not merely observers of experience; they are participants as well.

In spite of her fears the Lindberghs land safely, and soon the Japanese naval vessel *Shinshiru Maru* arrives to assist them with aircraft and engine repairs brought on as a result of their hard landing on the rough seas and the effects of the salt spray on the engine. Fog continued to interfere with their progress down the Japanese island chain, and they were forced to divert from their destination at Nemuro to a lake on Kunashiri Island, where they encountered a native fisherman and his family. The chapter that describes this meeting, "A Fisherman's Hut" (chapter 14), provides a kind of closure to their travels. In their attempt to communicate with the Japanese fisherman, they unfold their route map, hoping to convey some sense of who they are and why they have arrived unexpectedly out of the skies. After drawing a condensed version of their route of flight across Canada and Alaska they are able to establish one point of contact; the young boy recognizes the name *New York*: "'Ah!' cried the boy, his face lighting up with recognition, 'Noo Yawk!'" (179).

By that time my husband had finished his map. He set it down on the floor in our midst and pointed with his pencil, "New York—Canada—Alaska—Siberia—Chishima—Kunashiri—" of which they understood only New York and Kunashiri. Satisfied with our achievement, we put our wet feet up against the fire and all smiled. (179)

Their "achievement" is, on one level, success in communicating, however incompletely, with their hosts; on another level, however, the term also includes their truly remarkable achievement of completing a flight over the terrain they have marked out on the map. Their arrival in Japan marked the end of their travels over remote and isolated territory.

When they arrived in Tokyo, the Lindberghs kept a busy schedule, visiting the United States ambassador, the prime minister, and other dignitaries. The Lindberghs remained in Tokyo for two and a half weeks, from 26 August to 13 September. But of their extended stay in Tokyo, Lindbergh describes only one episode, a private visit to a tea garden, where she learns about the Japanese tea ceremony (chapter 15, "The Paper and String of Life"). This chapter, although not one of the longer chapters, is especially appealing for the series of descriptions of Japanese art and aesthetic values that it provides. The chapter describes a series of items Lindbergh sees during her stay in Tokyo: a paper umbrella, a fan, a painting. She looks "with wonder on the Japanese appreciation of all small things in nature" (186). She asks herself whether the Japanese, "from generations spent in one-story paper houses, [have] learned a language, an alphabet of beauty in nature, that we, in our houses of brick and stone, have shut out?" (187).

As she is shown a watercolor depicting a bird, some grass and flowers in one corner of the scroll, the remainder of the canvas being devoid of marks, she reflects that the empty portion of the canvas is "crowded with space," and that space is the most important part of the painting, "like those silences in a conversation which are so powerful that words against them flicker feebly, as stars against the wealth of blackness at night" (187).

Most of the chapter describes the Japanese Tea Ceremony as it is conducted in a tea house. The tea house is a special place, set apart from the house itself, where one goes with a small number of friends, to share the delight and intimacy of brewing and drinking tea. The features of the tea house are carefully chosen, and the few decorative elements are selected for their special value. The visit to the tea house sharpens Lindbergh's sense of aesthetic appreciation. She thinks to herself that if she could stay in Japan for a longer period of time, "I would learn to see too. And after minutely watching the surface of things I would learn to see below the surface" (193).

Lindbergh's descriptive powers would also be improved, she believes. She understands the full meaning of *simile* in the comparison of wet stones and new-peeled pears; she sees the value of *metaphor* in a reference to her young boy as a "hunter of the dragon fly"; and she appreciates the richness of *symbolism* when she learns that bamboo represents prosperity, the pine tree long life, and the plum tree courage "because the plum puts forth blossoms while the snow is still on the ground" (193). Her heightened sense of aesthetic appreciation is directly relevant to the process of recapturing the sights she has seen on her flight and conveying to her readers the importance and personal significance of those experiences. In "The Paper and String of Life" Lindbergh recognizes the elements of a language suitable for conveying the meanings of important experiences.

China and After

After a brief episode in which a Japanese youth attempts to hide inside the aircraft so that he might make his escape to America (chapter 16, "The Stowaway"), Lindbergh's travel account continues with five chapters describing their activities around and near their final stop, Nanking, China, where Charles is asked to assist in survey efforts over the flooding Yangtze River. The Lindberghs spent nearly two weeks in the Nanking area assisting Chinese authorities and the National Flood Relief Commission, mapping the flooded areas and transporting doctors and medical supplies. In Nanking Lindbergh is fascinated by the contrast of the old world of the walled city and the technological marvel of their modern aircraft (chapter 19, "The Wall of Nanking").

"The Most Beautiful Pagoda" (chapter 20) links her insights on perspective that she gained in Tokyo to the scenes she is witnessing during the flight. The chapter creates a vision of a pagoda over which they fly, whereby the whole becomes more than the sum of its parts, each part seen in isolation, a perspective achieved by the distancing effect of the atmospheric conditions:

Even the landscape seemed unreal, for in that late afternoon mist the hills and islands looked as they do in some of the old oriental scroll paintings—not placed according to the conventions of perspective, one behind another, but as though each were suspended, one above the other in some atmosphere, some wash all of the same tone. (223)

At this, the farthest point in their journey, Lindbergh is able to see the geographical features below "not placed according to the conventions of perspective," but separated from one another, each with its own sense of value and significance. According to her own account, she has been able to see and to describe the scenes of her flight against a new and more valuable perspective, in which each element is singled out and appreciated for its own value. It is not surprising, then, that she should see the pagoda as the symbolic goal of their flight, as the end point of her aesthetic discovery: "Centered like that, a gem in its frame, it gave one also an indescribable feeling of finality and peace, as though one had reached the end of the journey or come to the heart of some mystery" (223).

The vision of the pagoda involves the ability to see important events and scenes in two fashions simultaneously—in isolation, and as part of a larger continuum of experience. The actual end of the journey comes almost as an anticlimax, described in "Into the Yangtze" (chapter 21). The powers of nature, as represented in the turgid Yangtze, finally catch up with the Lindberghs and upset their technological miracle, the airplane, forcing them to abandon plans to continue the journey.

The tipping of the aircraft as it was being unloaded from the deck of the British aircraft carrier *Hermes* required both Lindberghs to jump into the river to avoid becoming trapped in the aircraft. Fortunately, both were rescued safely. Their immersion in the Yangtze provides the final lesson of the voyage, as they are literally baptized by experience.

The final chapter in the book, "Flying Again" (chapter 23), summarizes the lessons provided in the previous chapters and links past events to the future; the larger theme of *North to the Orient,* heightened perception, is again emphasized. The chapter recounts a flight that the Lindberghs made together several years later, from New York to Washington. On this flight, the landmarks that are passing underneath them are human landmarks: housing developments, tenements, parking lots, highways. But as she is observing these artificial patterns below, she recalls the "fundamental magic of flying," of the "miracle that has nothing to do with any of its practical purposes" (243). The magic results from the ability of flight to elevate one above the hectic pace of daily life, to see "life put in new patterns from the air" (244). Flying is magic, she concludes, because it can offer a vision "like a glass-bottomed bucket" which "can give you that vision, that seeing eye, which peers down to the still world below the choppy waves" (244). The concluding chapter returns the narrative from the past to the present, thus completing the plan of the thematic approach, to show how past events and present memories continually illuminate one another, but only when they are linked in the appropriate perspective.

Chapter Five
Listen! the Wind

Unlike *North to the Orient,* an outward-directed book, *Listen! the Wind* is inner-directed. This book devotes less time to an account of their travels than *North to the Orient,* describing people rather than country-side, exploring an inner landscape of emotions and anxieties. The two primal elements of wind and sea become major factors in the Lind-berghs' struggle to return to America, and the tension in the book results from their helplessness when these two elements work against them. There is also a detailed account of Lindbergh's radio-operating procedures, as she describes with obvious pleasure the sense of satisfaction she derived from her ability to transmit and receive information relevant to the progress of their flight across the Atlantic. Lindbergh's ability to communicate successfully provides her with a sense of confidence and security that is more than a footnote to the details of their flight; it is an important part of the ideas of shared experience and personal fulfillment that help to resolve the thematic crisis of the book. Saint-Exupéry thought this book a profound and moving document; linking external description to self-exploration, it may be Lindbergh's most successful literary achievement.

In the spring of 1933 the Lindberghs began planning their second extended overwater survey trip, one that would eventually take them to Greenland, Iceland, Scandinavia, Russia, Europe, Africa, and South America. While Lindbergh welcomed the chance of escape and change the trip offered, she did not anticipate it with the same excitement as she had in 1931. She must also have felt some anxieties at leaving her young second son behind during such a long trip, and thoughts of her distant son, the length of the trip, and the unwanted publicity in Europe combined to add to the fatigue she felt during the trip.

The Lindberghs left on the first leg of their trip on 9 July 1933, when they departed Flushing Bay, Long Island, for the Morrow sum-mer home on North Haven island, Maine, the same starting point of their first trip two years earlier. From North Haven they flew to Green-land, making en-route stops in Nova Scotia, Newfoundland, and Labrador. From 22 July until 15 August they conducted aerial surveys of the coast and interior of Greenland, assisted by a support crew aboard the Pan American Airways supply ship, the *Jelling.* They then journeyed to the Scandinavian countries via Iceland, the Faeroe Islands, and the Shetland Islands. From the end of August until the beginning of October they visited Denmark, Sweden, Finland, and Russia before flying to the British Isles for a three-week stay. Then followed brief stops in France, Holland, Switzerland, Spain, and Portugal.

The Lindberghs began the homeward leg of their trip on 21 November when they departed Lisbon, Portugal, for stops in the Azores and Canary Islands. Then, after a brief stop in Villa Cisneros on the northwest coast of Africa, they flew southwest to Santiago, in the Cape Verde Islands, which they hoped to use as their jumping-off place for the flight across the Atlantic to South America. But strong surface winds prevented them from taking off with the necessary fuel load, and they were forced to divert East, to Bathurst, Gambia, on the African coast.

At Bathurst calm weather prevented them from taking off with the full load of fuel required for the cross-ocean hop. Eventually, after Charles lightened their load by stripping unnecessary equipment and bracings from the aircraft, they were able to depart. After a flight of seventeen hours they landed safely at Natal, Brazil. The journey concluded with stops in Trinidad, Puerto Rico, Santo Domingo, and Miami. On 19 December 1933, they once again landed in Flushing Bay, Long Island.

During this six-month trip the Lindberghs made fifty-four stops in over twenty countries; their route extended over 30,000 air miles. Their Lockheed Sirius aircraft was donated to the American Museum of Natural History at the conclusion of their trip and was already on public display by the end of January 1934, a little over a month after their return. First built in 1929, the plane had become outmoded by newer aircraft designs. Later the aircraft was transferred to the Smithsonian Institution in Washington, D.C., where it was put on display in the National Air and Space Museum.

Flying Around the North Atlantic

Once again, as on the earlier journey, Lindbergh flew in the rear seat of the Lockheed Sirius amphibian aircraft, maintaining radio communications and helping with flying duties. In contrast to the previous trip, she wrote her notes in her diary as well as letters home. For this reason, perhaps, her trip notes for the 1933 flight are generally more detailed, more personal, and more revealing than are her 1931 observations.

Lindbergh intended to expand her trip notes into book form, but was prevented from doing so immediately by the need to finish the *North to the Orient* manuscript and by a commitment to *National Geographic Magazine* to prepare an article about the journey they had just completed. Lindbergh devoted relatively little time to writing the article; she worked on it during a two-week period in July 1934, after the first draft of *North to the Orient* had been written (*LR*, 192–93). The article, entitled "Flying Around the North Atlantic," was published in the September 1934 issue and was actually the first of Lindbergh's travel writings to be published, preceding *North to the Orient* by almost a year and *Listen! the Wind* by almost four years.

Lindbergh's preliminary account of their trip, "Flying Around the North Atlantic," is remarkable both for the detail of its seventy-eight-page narrative and the quality of the accompanying pictures, most of which were taken by the Lindberghs. Even though the *National Geographic* regularly published photo essays of aerial survey flights throughout the 1920s and 1930s, Lindbergh's article is exceptional for its narrative and pictorial detail. In Greenland the Lindbergh aircraft was finally christened; the local natives gave it the name *Tingmissartoq*, "the one who flies like a big bird." The name was painted on the side of the aircraft by a helpful young Greenland native (*LR*, 94).

Once the *National Geographic* article had been completed and the final draft of *North to the Orient* had been submitted, Lindbergh was ready to concentrate her energies on *Listen! the Wind*. But by that time it was September 1935; in December the Lindberghs moved to England in an attempt to find the privacy that had been denied them by the American press since the loss of their child in 1932.

The Structure of Experience

Lindbergh worked fairly intensively on the first draft of *Listen! the Wind* from March to June 1936. By January 1937 she estimated she was one third of the way through the draft (*FN*, 127). By January 1938 she had completed her first draft of *Listen! the Wind*; from then until the middle of June she reworked this and added a third section to the book, which she noted contained some "radio chapters" (*FN*,

229–30). She recorded in her diary that on 21 June, one day before her birthday, and in the midst of their move to France, she had finished the book (*FN*, 304). It was published by Harcourt, Brace, & Co. in September of that year. As he had for *North to the Orient*, Charles Lindbergh prepared the illustrations and dust jacket design.

Listen! the Wind is noticeably different in tone and scope from *North to the Orient*; readers who take up *Listen! the Wind* expecting the global panorama and cheerful approach of the earlier book are likely to be surprised at this book's limited scope of action and pensive mood. Whereas in *North to the Orient* each of the twenty-three chapters depicts different settings, events, and people, the thirty-three chapters of *Listen! the Wind* provide a continuous uninterrupted narrative of events that occurred during a ten-day period from 27 November to 6 December 1933. Instead of recapping the personal high points of the entire journey, as she did in *North to the Orient*, in *Listen! the Wind* Lindbergh restricts her vision to three seemingly unimportant segments of the trip, segments identified by the three named divisions of the book: "Santiago" (in the Cape Verde Islands); "Bathurst" (in Gambia, Africa); and "Bound Natal" (en route from Gambia to Natal, Brazil).

The first section, "Santiago," focuses on the lives and actions of the poor, young, sickness-afflicted station manager and his wife, caretakers of the all-but-abandoned seaplane base near Porto Praia, in the Cape Verde Islands. The young manager, who had been a radio operator for a French airline (probably *Aeropostale*, forerunner of *Air France*), is proud of his position, for one of his background (he is part black) would not normally be expected to hold a position of such importance. The station manager is clearly ill, as the Lindberghs quickly perceive, and the station mechanic tells them that the manager suffers from tuberculosis.

Lindbergh is fascinated by the quality of life of the young stationmaster and his wife, for she describes their residence, their appearance, their conversations, and their mannerisms in detail. Her account of their interaction with the illness-afflicted young couple contains elements of repulsion and attraction, giving rise to a curious push-pull effect in the narrative. The description of their first meal with the station manager and his wife illustrates the qualities of attraction and repulsion:

We were hungry and the food tasted good. The plates were clean, the table neat, but we were not at ease, not free to enjoy our supper or to talk spontaneously to our host. We were divided. It was as though we were only half there. Two people were there, sitting at the table, hungry, sympathetic, part of the group, inside the friendly circle. But there were two other people standing outside in the dark, looking in the lighted window—two outsiders, hostile, aloof, spying on that unconscious group around the table; watching the glasses to see if they were clean; watching the plates to see if they were washed; watching the napkins; watching the forks and spoons; whispering in the dark outside, "Tout est contaminé, tout est sale."

It was a silent meal. The smell of roasting coffee was pungent and delicious. The "Chef" [Manager] coughed occasionally. (*LW,* 56–57)

The new kind of danger, disease, is opposed to an obvious sense of sympathy with their hosts. The writing is especially vivid, reflecting her feeling of awkwardness and discomfort, caused as much by her social conditioning as by the physical conditions in which they find themselves. Lindbergh seems to be drawn out of herself and involved—perhaps involuntarily—in the lives of the earnest but afflicted young couple. In "Santiago" there is no attempt to present a cheerful travelogue of the kind found in *North to the Orient*; her writing here conveys weariness and discomfort.

The second section, "Bathurst," chronicles their preparations for departure to South America from Gambia, and the tone of the book begins to return to the more positive mood of *North to the Orient*. Although Lindbergh describes many of the details of the lives and activities of their hosts at Bathurst, she is not really interested in their personalities nor their tasks; in this section her primary focus is upon their aircraft.

When they are unsuccessful in their attempts to depart for South America, Lindbergh wonders if their airplane, which has carried them safely over much of the earth's surface, is beginning to fail them. At the outset of their first attempt to depart Bathurst, early in the morning of their third day, Lindbergh notices that they are so heavily loaded that their pontoons are at times almost submerged by the wash of the waves. She imagines the fatigue of the aircraft:

The plane began to nose out toward the open bay, leaving the small cove, the docks and buoys behind, but so slowly and heavily, heaving from side to side as it pushed across waves in the current. It had never felt like this before. It actually seemed to creak, tired and lumbering, like a fat old woman puffing up stairs. Could this be our swift and powerful machine? (160)

Then comes the takeoff attempt; Lindbergh vividly describes the experiences she and her husband felt on every takeoff they made from a water surface:

Blast of noise, rush of spray, storming over us, throbbing in our ears, streaming over the pontoons, the wings, the cockpits, pounding through the seats. Maelstrom of sound and spray, both inextricably mixed in a roar of power, covered us completely, enclosed us, cut us off from the world. No sound outside the engine's blast; no sight beyond the wall of spray. We were wrapped in the curl of a wave; we were poised in the heart of a typhoon. (162)

Their heavy weight and the lack of wind prevented a successful takeoff, and they were forced to return to the Governor's residence until weather conditions improved.

Prior to their third takeoff attempt, on the evening of 5 December, Lindbergh describes her efforts to prepare herself spiritually for their flight while her husband prepares the aircraft. She scans the bay for signs of a helping breeze and reads poetry, finding particular solace in Humbert Wolfe's "Autumn Resignation," from which the title of the book—"Listen! the wind is rising. . . ."—is taken (204–05). The passage that describes their successful launch graphically depicts the struggle and release from their earth- and water-bound condition:

We are spanking along. We are up on the step—faster, faster—oh, much faster than before. Sparks from the exhaust. We're going to get off! . . . Yes—we're off—we're rising. . . . We turn from the lights of the city; we pivot on a dark wing; we roar over the earth. The plane seems exultant now, even arrogant. (216–17)

In this description the aircraft has imaginatively shaken off its lethargy and has regained its former vitality. This passage closely parallels the original description in Lindbergh's diary (*LR*, 170); the sense of release evident in the final takeoff from Africa for the return to the American continent is the central emotional event of the book.

In the third section of the book, "Bound Natal," the events described are limited to the interior of the aircraft and to the rear seat—Lindbergh's airborne working environment—as she concentrates intensely on her duties as a radio operator. These final six chapters of *Listen! the Wind* give us the most detailed account of Lindbergh's radio communication tasks to be found in her travel writings. There are two likely reasons for this detailed description: one reason is that at the time during which she was writing this section (the spring of 1938), she could have sensed that her days as a radio operator on world survey flights were finished—at least in the *Tingmissartoq*, for by then the aircraft was on display in a museum. But more important, this leg, from Bathurst to Natal, was the longest overwater flight she had flown with her husband on any of their aerial travels. While it was not as long a flight as her husband's 1927 flight from New York to Paris, it nevertheless was a sixteen-hour flight, and continuous radio communication was essential to its safe conclusion.

The first of the six chapters of the third section, "My Little Room," is a nine-page description of the rear-seat environment of the Lockheed Sirius aircraft; it provides a complete and detailed account of the many instruments, control levers, and mechanisms that Lindbergh was responsible for monitoring or operating during the course of the flight. The tone of the description is warm and personal. Her affectionate account was probably due to the fact that she had seen many unusual sights and had worked diligently as a productive crew member in this small space. Her pride in her work and her familiarity with her working station were the result of many hours of time spent in her "little room," as she calls it.

This chapter was written later, in retrospect, and the account serves at least partially as a tribute to the aircraft that had borne her and her husband with exceptional safety and reliability across large portions of the earth's surface. Lindbergh's detailed description of the rear cockpit (223–27) is prefaced with this summarizing comment on its special significance to her:

This little cockpit of mine became extraordinarily pleasing to me, as much so as a furnished study at home. Every corner, every crack, had significance. Every object meant something. Not only the tools I was working with, the transmitter and receiver, the key and the antenna reel; but even the small irrelevant objects on the side of the fuselage, the little black hooded light, its face now turned away from me, the shining arm and knob of the second throttle, the bright switches and handles, the colored wires and copper pipes: all gave me, in a strange sense, as much pleasure as my familiar books and pictures might at home. The pleasure was perhaps not esthetic but came from a sense of familiarity, security, and possession. I invested them with an emotional significance of their own, since they had been through so much with me. They made up this comfortable, tidy, compact world that was mine. (222–23)

Lindbergh saw this restricted space as a safe and comfortable operating environment. Its appeal was undoubtedly due to the fact that, in a life of world travel, it provided an unchanging habitat. In addition, the passage indicates the human capacity to accommodate itself to a technological environment. The comfort of the aircraft surroundings results in part from confidence in knowing the specialized names and operations of the machinery: cockpit, transmitter, receiver, antenna reel, fuselage, throttle.

After the Lindberghs landed on the river at Natal, Brazil, their flight to South America was over. Although the journey back to Flushing Bay on Long Island was not completed for another two weeks, emotionally, if not geographically, Lindbergh's journey was at an end.

Symbol and Theme

At first glance it appears that *Listen! the Wind* consists of three separate, very different sections, linked only by their chronological sequence. However, the three sections are unified by symbols of wind and time and by the theme of restriction and release. Throughout the book the wind is a symbol of the one force of nature essential to their success in aerial exploration. Like all natural forces, the wind is unpredictable and inconsistent, alternately assisting and hindering their progress:

The wind—which one can never count on, which sometimes, bearing down on one wing or on another, lures one imperceptibly out of one's course. Or, towering in one's face, makes the flight a long uphill climb, draining away the precious daylight, devouring the fuel. This wind, usually so perverse, uncontrollable, and fickle, had been ours for two thousand miles. (4)

When they land near Porto Praia, the wind becomes an antagonistic presence, blowing with excessive strength, forcing them to delay their flight home. It becomes a dominating force, imprisoning them against their will: "But it did not seem like wind. . . . It was more like a great river, a wave, which drowned the hill, and sheathed the island. And we, caught at the bottom of it, were struggling to swim against the current" (40). Then, at Bathurst, when they are unable to become airborne for a lack of wind, Lindbergh reflects, "Daybreak—dusk, moonrise—moonset, light—darkness: all these factors sank to secondary importance, subject to that one vital element over which we had no control—wind (170)." When they finally arrive in Natal, exhausted but relieved, Lindbergh notes with pleasure that they are once again favored with a beneficial wind (262).

The wind represents other forces than the forces of nature; it functions as an emotional signpost, reflecting the narrator's frame of mind. In Porto Praia the wind is a hard and incessant force, producing physical strain and feverish conditions linked to the disease they find there; in Bathurst it is calm, and Lindbergh is able to compose herself for the flight to America; during the flight across it is associated with electrical storms, as she manipulates certain electrical components of the aircraft to obtain needed information on the radio. The wind is also the element most directly associated with the success of their flight, for their aircraft depends on aerodynamic forces for lift and propulsion, and a favorable wind will extend their range.

The wind is related to time, also; this connection is most evident in the Porto Praia section, when Lindbergh feels isolated from time by the wind:

The wind had not stopped. . . . Hurry, hurry, hurry, it seemed to say, as though there were not time enough to reach the places one must reach—not time enough to finish all the work one had to do. . . . Time didn't count here at all. It had stopped. (48–49)

Once they arrive safely in Gambia, she feels they have returned to a more regular time system: "Life was going on here; it meant something. Time counted; we were in the stream again" (125). En route to Natal, the passage of time is a measure of the progress of the flight; as each hour passes, their location must be noted and their position reported. Time and their movement forward are inextricably linked; the feeling of being apart from time is gone.

The Porto Praia episode, the depiction of the station manager and his wife, is the central section of the book. It is the longest of the three sections and contains the most additional detail, the most supplementary material added to the basic diary entries. Its importance to Lindbergh is evident in a consideration of her presentation of the lives of the young couple, the station manager and his wife. The descriptions of the pressure of the wind, the hot, dry conditions, and her sense of entrapment during their stay at Porto Praia may well reflect her own weariness and despair, due not only to the length of the trip but also to the events of her life from 1932 to 1935. These events affected her mood during the trip and the tone of her writing in *Listen! the Wind*.

The sense of emotional pressure the book conveys is reinforced by the increasingly restricted sense of perspective experienced by the narrator in the three episodes of the book. They reveal a gradual movement toward confinement, as Lindbergh begins by describing events external to their operation in the aircraft, in the "Porto Praia" section, and then focuses more intensely on the aircraft itself in the "Bathurst" section. Then, in the final section, "Bound Natal," the narrated events take place entirely within the space of the aircraft cockpit. When the aircraft comes in sight of the S. S. *Westfalen*, off the coast of South America, the overwhelming sense of relief at the completion of the overwater passage suggests that the emotionally draining pressures of the journey are about to be released.

Saint-Exupéry was one of the first readers to respond to the sense of emotional pressure and fatigue that the book conveyed; in his preface to the French edition, he noted that he sensed "a faint anguish suffusing these pages. It takes different forms, but it circulates tirelessly through the book like a silent blood stream" (*A Sense of Life,* 172). Saint-Exupéry also noted Lindbergh's preoccupation with time: "for them time must be set in motion again. They must rejoin the continent, reenter the stream, return to where men are worked hard, where they can change and be alive" (174). Saint-Exupéry's compliment to Lindbergh also catches the spirit of the book: "It is an extraordinary revelation to see this kind of inner anxiety in a couple whom the whole world has applauded" (174).

Similar in structure and content, *North to the Orient* and *Listen! the Wind* differ significantly in mood, tone, and theme. The Anne Morrow Lindbergh of *North to the Orient* is exuberant, excited, and innocent, and the airplane in which she and her husband travel is a kind of time-and-space machine that brings new and unknown worlds to them at a rapid rate. The Anne Morrow Lindbergh of *Listen! the Wind* is cautious, pensive, and experienced, and their airplane is now a protective chamber to which she can escape from the inexorable pressures of the world through which they must make their way. The airplane is a vehicle for outward discovery on *North to the Orient* and a vehicle for inner discovery in *Listen! the Wind.*

Chapter Six
The Wave of the Future

Probably none of Anne Morrow Lindbergh's books has been the subject of more argument, criticism, and misunderstanding than her third book, *The Wave of the Future*. This small forty-one-page book produced a tremendously animated public response; evidence of one aspect of the book's influence can be seen today in repeated uses of the phrase "wave of the future," often used in connection with the development of some new product or technological breakthrough. But most people who use the phrase are probably not aware of its origin. Written primarily as Lindbergh's attempt to clarify in her own mind her rationale for American noninvolvement in the war on the European continent, *The Wave of the Future* became a focal point of the debate over neutrality versus direct involvement in the months before the Japanese attack on Pearl Harbor. Its antiwar, noninvolvement sentiment evolved, in part, from her response to her husband's isolationist speeches in the early months of World War II. But it also owed its genesis to the philosophical views of her father, Dwight Morrow, primarily his middle-of-the-road, practical approach to solving international disputes. Although Lindbergh later expressed regret for some of the views presented in the book, *The Wave of the Future* nevertheless remains a significant literary achievement because it was written during an important moment in American history, and because it represents an essential expression of the rational outlook that pervades her writing.

In spite of the work's stronger appeal to emotion than to fact, Lindbergh articulated in a calm and persuasive manner thoughts that were on the minds of many Americans in late 1940, by arguing that the conflict in Europe was more than a simplistic confrontation of the forces of Good and Evil. In addition to a quiet and reasoned style, she incorporated natural elements as symbols, including the sea and features of the American landscape. In *The Wave of the Future* Lindbergh worked toward a goal that was probably impossible to attain, but she achieved an impressive level of success.

The Wave of the Future is the central, keystone document in a three-part statement of Lindbergh's fears of and reactions to the early events of World War II. Her initial views of the war in Europe appeared in an article entitled "Prayer for Peace," published in the *Reader's Digest* in January 1940. *The Wave of the Future* was published in October of that year. Her third statement, "Reaffirmation," a response to critics of *The Wave of the Future,* appeared in the *Atlantic Monthly* in June 1941. The three works are integrally linked; to consider *The Wave of the Future* in an appropriate context it is necessary to consider the three essays as a whole and to review the events in the Lindberghs' lives and world conditions that preceded the writing of these three sequential works.

Background

Charles Lindbergh's knowledge of German aircraft production capacities gained during his and his wife's three-and-a-half year stay in Europe made him fearful of German technological superiority, and he despaired of a peaceful outcome of the European political situation. Anne, who accompanied him on many of his trips, came to share these views from her own observations and from discussions with her husband and the people they met on their travels. Within five months after their return to the United States, Germany invaded Poland, and the war they had been dreading began. From the fall of 1939 until the attack on Pearl Harbor in December 1941, Charles was involved in nonintervention activities, giving thirteen addresses across the country and becoming allied with the America First Committee.

In April he resigned his commission in the Air Corps, a move prompted by his desire not to bring adverse publicity upon his friends in the military service, and by his repeated attacks on President Roosevelt's foreign policy. On 11 September in a speech at Des Moines, Iowa, he addressed some of his remarks toward American Jews, suggesting that they were pressuring the administration into involvement in the war to serve their own interests. These remarks brought a great outcry against him, so intense that even some of his hard-line conservative friends on the America First Committee began to distance themselves from him.

Anne shared her husband's concern over German war preparedness, but was not by nature an isolationist in her views as was her husband.

Her educational and literary inclinations led her toward a more universal perspective. While she was willing to believe that the United States was largely unprepared for involvement in the war, she was less enthusiastic about nonintervention. As a result of her wide reading and the many personal contacts the Lindberghs had made during their stay in Europe, she was reluctant to speak out for the kind of position that her husband had taken, a position that appeared to counsel turning a deaf American ear to the plight of their European friends. Thus torn between two opposing stands—one in favor of nonintervention, the other of sympathy and support for England and France—she began to work out a philosophical position that she hoped would accommodate both views. Her trilogy conveying her concern over world affairs—the three works mentioned above, with *The Wave of the Future* as the cornerstone—was the result.

Part 1: "A Prayer for Peace"

"A Prayer for Peace" is aptly named, for it is an extended meditation and deeply felt hope for peace in Europe. It contains ideas and attitudes that Lindbergh had been nurturing for a number of months, ideas and attitudes that reflected her profound despair over the European situation, ideas and attitudes shared by many Americans. The news of the German invasion of Poland created a particularly deep distress for Lindbergh; in her diary entry at that time she compared her response to the German invasion to the sense of loss she felt when her child had been taken: "The child is dead. The child is dead in Europe" (*WW,* 44). She also records that she has been praying, in the same way she had when her son was taken (*WW,* 46).

This profound personal unhappiness lies at the core of her motivation for writing her noninterventionist works. Her anger at the fact of the war prompted her to write a first draft of "A Prayer for Peace" quickly, in a little less than a month, in October 1939: "Hours I spent writing—passionately, all I felt about the war—then seeing that it was bitter and realizing I must cut all the bitterness out of it and seeing that it was also not well founded enough or documented enough (the history part—no one would listen to a dreamer and a 'poet' on the causes of the war) . . ." (*WW,* 65).

Lindbergh begins "A Prayer for Peace" by admitting her limitations as an authority on the subject for which she speaks: she acknowledges that she is a woman speaking about what are commonly thought of as men's issues in a man's world. But, she continues, her need to communicate her feelings is much greater than her ability to remain silent: "I write because I feel these things so passionately that I must cry out" ("Prayer for Peace," *Reader's Digest* 36 [January 1940], 1–2). Convinced that there are others who share her views, she says that it is these people to whom she wishes to "speak for a patient, persistent, intelligent, long-range attitude toward peace" (2).

Having established her theme, Lindbergh then reviews the issues she sees associated with it: it is not too late to promote peace (the war was four months old when the article appeared), and the United States should use restraint in the way in which it encourages the Allies to fight. She argues that the United States should let the Allies fight the war in the best way they know how, and she reminds her readers that the United States contributed to the European crisis, first, by agreeing to the unfair peace terms inflicted on Germany after the end of World War I, and second, by the American failure to support the League of Nations, the one means by which European security might have been attained. The best stand America can take, she argues, is to help ameliorate the conditions of war and not to aggravate them.

Lindbergh acknowledges that the Nazi regime has used force with awful effect, but she sees the spirit of "Hitlerism" as the direct manifestation of the deep-seated distress of post-World War I Germany. She identifies one of the causes of the European conflict as the dissatisfaction in the German people, in "the spirit of an embittered Germany" (4). The calm logic of these ideas, perhaps more than any other aspect of the essay, spoke most effectively to the American audience. These ideas, much expanded, constituted the central theme of *The Wave of the Future*.

Lindbergh argues that the only victor of a protracted European conflict will be Russia and that all other European countries will suffer. After painting a despairing picture of the effect of the war on Europe, she urges the establishment of peace, a peace based at first on an uneasy armed truce, but one that could lead to resolution of the causes of the strife, assisted by science and compassion. Lest she be accused of providing an accommodation of German demands, she states that she is not a pacifist, but is motivated instead by her vision of a new order, one which will prevent the resurgence of the spirit of "Hitlerism" (7).

"The Prayer for Peace" presents the central ideas that form the basis of the subsequent essay, when "the spirit of Hitlerism" grows into— but is not the same thing as—the "wave of the future." We can also begin to appreciate the narrow philosophical path she set herself on when she undertook these essays. On the one hand, she wanted to point to what she felt were the probable and unhappy causes of the German uprising without defending German military aggression. On the other hand, she wanted to urge American caution and introspection to avoid unthinking involvement—in what must necessarily become a very destructive war—without seeming to ignore entirely the needs of and close cultural affinities with the English and French. This combination of personal interest and political realities made it practically impossible for Lindbergh to walk this narrow path successfully. Yet her intense idealism, her close personal familiarity with the European situation, and her natural inclination for peaceful resolution (qualities she shared with her husband) led her to continue determinedly along the difficult path she had marked for herself.

"A Prayer for Peace" was well received by American (and even English) readers, for in the essay Lindbergh had voiced a common hope— that peace could still be obtained (*WW,* 78). This response, this continuing hope, was not surprising considering the fact that diplomatic efforts to maintain peace in response to German demands had been an established pattern in world affairs for over two years. Her essay appeared at a time favorable to prospects for peace, in January 1940, during the relative calm of the "Phoney War," before the German armies invaded France. When the war moved into its next phase, after the fall of France, and during the Battle of Britain, Lindbergh could no longer practically pray for world peace. But she could urge Americans to reflect on their social ideals and philosophies, and this she did in *The Wave of the Future.*

Part 2: The Keystone Document

In late May 1940 Lindbergh wrote a long letter to her former teacher of creative writing at Smith College, Mina Curtiss. After discussing the challenges and difficulties of writing, she reflected on the world condition: "The wave that is sweeping over Europe will, it seems to me, surely sweep over us too. I don't mean necessarily war or Nazi domination. But, rather, something else which is trying to push up through the crust of the world's habits and has thus far only found its expression in such horrible and abortive forms as communism, nazism, and war" (*WW,* 93).

Four months later this comment was given greater articulation in
The Wave of the Future, a work that disturbed the already troubled
minds of Americans. *The Wave of the Future* is an expanded version of
the thought Lindbergh shared with her former teacher; but it became
one of the most widely discussed books to appear during the course of
the war.

According to her diary, Lindbergh wrote *The Wave of the Future* in a
ten-day period, from 16 to 25 August 1940. This was not her normal
mode of writing, which was to work and rework her material over an
extended period of time. A diary entry dated 16 August, when the
aerial Battle of Britain was at its most crucial stage, suggests the reason
for the rapidity with which she worked: "I work on an article [*The
Wave of the Future*] all morning. I do not 'write' it exactly, I am so full
of it (the whole winter's travail of thought, anguish, doubt, arguments, defense—and affirmation). It flows out of me, unmindful of
how it is 'written'" (*WW,* 137). As her earlier comments to Mina Curtiss indicate, the ideas of *The Wave of the Future* had in fact been for-
mulating themselves in her mind for many months.

The essay begins on the same note of philosophical questioning that
characterized "A Prayer for Peace." She emphasizes that her essay is to
be thought of as a "confession of faith" (the subtitle of the book), and
she suggests that a faith "is not seen, but felt; not proved, but believed;
not a program, but a dream" (*WF,* 7).

Addressing the key question of whether involvement with the Allied
cause is as clear-cut a case of good against evil as the pro-Ally forces
argue, she suggests that such a perspective may be too simplistic in its
outlook, and that while the aggressions of the German forces may be
"sins," there are "other sins, such as blindness, selfishness, irresponsi-
bility, smugness, lethargy, and resistance to change—sins which we
'Democracies,' all of us, are guilty of" (11–12).

Lindbergh returns to an idea that appeared also in "A Prayer for
Peace," as she argues that the democracies could be accused of not
acting in good faith toward the German people after World War I, and
that if support instead of penalties had been extended to Germany there
might have been "no Naziism and no war" (13). Borrowing an image
from Yeats's "The Second Coming," she suggests that something important and ultimately valuable is "trying to come to birth" even
though its first appearance may take an unpleasant shape (15–16). She
characterizes the nationalist, expansionist movements at work in Ger-

many, Italy, and Russia as parts of a "vast revolution," whose forces and effects represent something larger than the struggle between the agents of good and evil (17). The leaders of these countries, she says, have discovered how to use the new social and economic forces that have surged up in the world. These forces may have been misused, but the leaders of Germany, Italy, and Russia "have sensed the changes and they have exploited them. They have felt the wave of the future and they have leapt upon it. The evils we deplore in these systems are not in themselves the future; they are scum on the wave of the future" (19). She urges her readers to take a larger, "planetary" view of the world's troubles, and to avoid moving toward pro- or antiwar positions in reaction to the "gigantic specter of fear" which exists in America (28–30).

Asking her readers to consider the dangerous conditions that helped to produce the war as a threat as serious as that of military invasion, Lindbergh returns to her metaphor of the sea to suggest the hopelessness of struggling against the forces of change at work in the world: "The wave of the future is coming and there is no fighting it" (37). She recommends reconsideration of personal and national value systems instead of marshaling for war. She challenges her readers to consider the merits of adapting to change, for, she says, "only in growth, reform, and change, paradoxically enough, is true security to be found" (38). She expresses the hope that change can occur without "such terrible bloodshed" as is occurring in Europe (39).

She closes by urging her readers to accept the "tremendous challenge" of bringing this dream of change "to birth in a warlike world," for, she concludes, "like all acts of creation it will take labor, patience, pain—and an infinite faith in the future" (40–41). Her comparison of her dream of change to the process of birth was more than a literary device; shortly after *The Wave of the Future* was published she gave birth to her fourth child—her first daughter.

Public reaction to *The Wave of the Future* was mixed and intense. Those who disagreed with its message often misread or misinterpreted certain key passages in the text, primarily those in which the expression "the wave of the future" appeared. In the essay Lindbergh specifically identifies the wave of the future with the widespread force of revolution at work in the world, not with the individual national movements, such as fascism, Nazism, and communism; these, she makes repeatedly clear, are the "scum" on the surface of the wave. But a common reaction was to argue that Lindbergh had identified Nazism

and fascism as the "wave of the future," and that she was urging submission to their programs of expansion. This misreading of her essay
appeared in numerous forms in the months following its publication;
even E. B. White's thoughtful and generally insightful review in *Harper's Magazine* in February 1941 illustrated this tendency.

Part 3: "Reaffirmation"

In a diary entry for 8 April 1941 Lindbergh notes that she has been
reading over her "old notes, including my 'answer' to my critics. Wish
now I had published it—and the thought disturbs my morning" (*WW*,
170). Because this is her first mention of any "reply" to critics of *The
Wave of the Future,* we can assume that she must have been mulling
over her reaction to critics for a number of months. A diary entry for
27 October 1940 recorded the comfort she received from a sympathetic
letter from the poet W. H. Auden, who wrote to her that "the hardest
solitude to bear" is "the knowledge that everything one writes goes out
helpless into the world to be turned to evil as well as good" (*WW*,
149). On 14 April 1941 she noted that her husband thought she
should publish her reply; two weeks later it was in the hands of the
Atlantic Monthly editors. It appeared in the June issue of the magazine
under the title "Reaffirmation."

The tone of "Reaffirmation" is stronger, more confident, than that
of the previous essays. Gone is Lindbergh's need to apologize for speaking out on the issue of world peace. Her aim now is not to lay the
foundation of a new philosophy, but to clarify her previously expressed
argument. She begins by reminding her readers that *The Wave of the
Future* was written not as a political pamphlet but as an expression of
her personal philosophy, and that some commonly voiced objections to
the essay need to be answered. The most troublesome aspect expressed
by her critics is their almost universal misreading of her metaphorical
use of the image of the *wave*; the wave, she says, was intended to
represent the force of change. But in the minds of many readers, she
continues, it has become a "protean symbol which has been used to
mean whatever the critic desires" ("Reaffirmation," *Atlantic Monthly*
167 [June 1941], 682). She denies that she ever associated it with the
Nazi, fascist, or communist movements: "To me, the Wave of the Future is none of these things. It is, as I see it, a movement of adjustment
to a highly scientific, mechanized, and material era of civilization,
with all its attendant complications, and as such it seems to me inev-

itable" (682). She repeats her description of the evils of fascism and Nazism as the "scum" on the surface of the wave, and she argues that her intent was not to suggest giving way before the wave but to prepare for it and to guide its forces in the best way possible (683).

In this clarification, and in the comments that follow, Lindbergh emphasizes the impact of *science* and *mechanization* much more heavily than she had in the earlier two essays. The causes of the current world-wide upheaval, she now says, are due as much to the effects of science and mechanization as to post-World War I economic conditions: "The causes, it seems to me, go back to actions of our own in the last century, to the impact of science on the delicately balanced life of man" (683). In this section Lindbergh demonstrates for the first time her concern about the problem of appropriate social accommodation of technological developments. She restates her idea that the present period is "revolutionary," adding that she believes that this revolution is "in its essence good" because "the effort to adjust to a mechanized world is a necessary one" (683).

Lindbergh restates at some length her belief that America should avoid involvement in the war in Europe because America is in a state of "internal and external unpreparedness" (684). Her stronger nonintervention message in "Reaffirmation" may be partly the result of her husband's intensive speech-making activities at the time.

Lindbergh closes by returning to her assessment of the causes of the current world revolution, in which she sees the advances of science and the emphasis on material things as important factors:

> The revolution that will have to take place over the world before it can again begin its march forward seems to me not alone the conquest of machine by man, but much more deeply the conquest of spirit over matter. The material world has outstripped us, and we must try to make up our lost ground. (686)

She concludes by suggesting that "we have in our heritage and in our temperament both the man of action and the dreamer; both the practical man and the visionary, the technician and the mystic," qualities that she hopes will enable America to "give her greatest possible contribution to civilization" (686).

In her 1940 and 1941 essays Lindbergh was fighting a losing battle against the American mood and world events. But these noninterventionist writings, and *The Wave of the Future* in particular, are significant in terms of what they represented to the American public at large and what they tell us about Lindbergh as a writer. *The Wave of the Future*—and to a lesser extent the two essays that precede and follow it—is significant because it reflects American confusion and concern over events in Europe. It attempts to articulate the conflicting feelings of revenge and guilt in regard to initial German aggression. It draws attention to the real need to avoid hasty and unthinking movement toward entering a war that America was, in 1939 and 1940, at least, ill prepared to wage. And it represents a significant rhetorical achievement in that it is able to present successfully a philosophically complex argument to an audience who received those arguments sympathetically (for the most part), even if it did not always agree with the viewpoints presented. *The Wave of the Future* both participates in and symbolizes a central intellectual issue at a crucial time in American history.

As a result of writing these essays, Lindbergh increased her commitment to social and political issues, strengthened her tendencies to describe personal growth, added dimensions of religious and spiritual elements to her writing, and confirmed her preference for images and metaphors of nature—especially of the wind and the sea. Even though she later abjured some of the ideas in and motivations for *The Wave of the Future*, it is in many ways the pivotal work of her creative career, generated in the crucible of personal commitment and public clamor.

Chapter Seven
The Steep Ascent

The Steep Ascent, published in 1944, is different from yet similar to Lindbergh's earlier flying narratives, *North to the Orient* and *Listen! the Wind.* Its most obvious difference is that it is cast in fictional form; unlike the earlier two books, it is not presented as a travel narrative. The flight that occurs in the novel is not a global jaunt to Greenland or the Orient, but a relatively common nonstop flight from England to Italy. There are no illuminating sketches of native people or unusual places; instead, the novel consists of a series of thoughts, reflections, and recollections in the mind of the narrator and primary figure of the book, Eve Alcott.

Alcott serves as a representative woman trying to establish a successful life for herself as a wife and mother, and the flight she shares with her fictional husband, Gerald, suggests the progress of their life from the comfort of domestic security to the danger of physical and intellectual overreaching. Lost in the clouds and fog of emotional and spiritual disorientation, the Alcotts safely descend over a calm sea. In this, the third of her trilogy of flight chronicles, the landscape of the flight is a symbolic, cultural landscape; *The Steep Ascent* describes a spiritual, not a geographical, flight.

Lindbergh's first attempt at fiction, *The Steep Ascent* does not appear to fulfill many of the requirements for standard works of fiction: it offers little plot development, few characters, and almost no dialogue. But it is not her intent to write a conventional story; it is essentially a variation on Lindbergh's preferred mode of discourse, the philosophical essay.

The Original Flight

The flight that served as the genesis for *The Steep Ascent* occurred in February and March 1937, when Lindbergh and her husband traveled from England to Italy and eventually to India. The trip was unlike their other extended flights, for in this instance the Lindberghs flew over heavily populated areas (for the most part), along well-established air routes. The trip itself attracted no special recognition, other than the attention the Lindberghs normally received whenever they traveled. They were not out to survey new air routes but were instead taking a modified vacation trip. They traveled this time in a recently acquired Miles Mohawk, a British-built two-seat monoplane which, like their Lockheed Sirius, featured a similar front- and rear-cockpit arrangement under a closed canopy.

They took off from Reading, England, just after 8:00 in the morning, flew over Long Barn to wave good-bye to their son Jon and his nursemaid, then landed at Lympne to clear English customs and to refuel. After a short delay waiting for the customs officer to arrive, they departed Lympne (located on the coast south of Dover), flew across the English Channel, over Reims in France, Neuchatel in Switzerland, and then across the Alps into northern Italy; their destination was Rome.

Once across the highest part of the Alps, they encountered clouds and fog; they lost all visual contact with the ground and were unable to determine their exact location. Charles eventually decided that their best hope for extricating themselves from the situation was to enter a slow, controlled, spiral descent into the clouds, hoping that the ceiling of the clouds beneath them would be high enough above the ground to allow them to avoid any trees or hills and to make their way safely into a local airport. Their situation was compounded by the fact that they were running low on fuel, it was growing dark, and one of their important aircraft instruments—the artificial horizon—had failed. These are Anne's impressions of the descent as she recorded them in her diary later:

Down, down into the darkness, but so gently. I never thought meeting death would be so quiet and so gentle. Slow, strange descent into the underworld. But while accepting, sinking into this featherlike descent, somehow I was watching every second with every inch of concentration, watching the spin of the low wing for what it would show. It would be death or escape and life for us both. (*FN*, 136)

Fortunately, they descended safely through the clouds and found themselves over the Mediterranean Sea off the coast of Genoa. Exhausted by their experience, they decided to land at nearby Pisa instead of proceeding to Rome, their intended stop.

The events of their one-day flight, which are described in six pages in *The Flower and the Nettle*, are developed into 120 pages in *The Steep Ascent*. However, seven years passed before the book based on the 1937 flight appeared. The forces responsible for its slow genesis included the onset of the war, the Lindberghs' noninterventionist activities, and their meeting with Antoine de Saint-Exupéry.

Genesis and Theme

In contrast to her earlier works on flying, *The Steep Ascent* was written relatively rapidly. Her diary entries show seven references to working on the novel, from 17 November 1942 through 14 March 1943, indicating that Lindbergh completed her first draft in about four months. In August she sent the manuscript to Harcourt, Brace, her usual publishers, with a letter in which she said that "I tried to put into it—a kind of final record—everything that a life of flying taught me, as though it were a final testament" (*WW*, 381–82). Harcourt, Brace suggested some minor revisions in the text. A revised manuscript was mailed to them on 18 October, on the same day, she notes in her diary, that sixty B-17s (600 men) were reported lost on a raid over Germany (*WW*, 391). *The Steep Ascent* was published in the first week of March 1944.

In its plot *The Steep Ascent* closely follows the events of the Lindberghs' 1937 flight. But in the thoughts and sensations of Eve Alcott, Lindbergh presents a complex study of a woman's sense of loss, fear, and renewal in the face of life-threatening conditions. As the story opens, Eve is hesitant to leave her young son and the security of her comfortable English home. She is especially reluctant because she does not like having to say "good-bye" (the title of Chapter 1), and because she is five months pregnant, as Anne Lindbergh was at the time of their 1937 flight. The juxtaposition of Eve's pregnancy and the hazards of flight establishes a basis for the emotional and thematic impact of the flight and the story, in which birth and death are linked. "Pregnancy was like old age, she reflected; and waiting for birth was like waiting for death. It was inevitable but unpredictable. It was common as earth and magnificent as sky. And though it happened to everyone you had to go through it stark alone" (*SA*, 15–16).

A sense of the pressure of time is also established in the opening chapters; in order to cross the Alps before dark and arrive in Italy on schedule, they must depart early and clear English customs quickly,

and hope that clear weather and favorable winds will assist their progress. Realizing that their departure from the English coast has been
delayed by an hour, Eve reflects on the nature of time in terms of the
primary metaphor that appears throughout the story—time as fabric:

A whole hour—it could never be mended. They would just have to get on
with the torn day as best they could. What a delicate fabric it was—Time.
How easily it got soiled or ripped. . . . How vulnerable one was cloaked in
such a garment, dependent on it. No one knew, but those who wore it, how
vulnerable one was. (39)

The first portion of the book identifies the issues and the themes which
the second portion amplifies. The issues evolve as the aircraft flies over
visually significant landmarks on its planned route. The first landmark
is the English Channel, a geographical feature that separates the old,
comfortable, familiar environment of England from the new and lesser
known Continent and the Alps. Their next significant landmark is the
World-War-I battlefield area along the Somme River and Cambrai. As
they pass over, Eve meditates on the courage of the men who must
fight a war from the trenches. The chapter clearly seems to recognize
the current struggle in Europe as well as the previous war. Eve recalls
her first meeting with Gerald at the Cleveland Air Races, an event in
which Charles Lindbergh had participated in 1929, and she likens Gerald's "gallantry" to the courage of the English officers of World War I.
As she recalls Gerald's apparently casual attitude toward the hazards of
flight, she again is reminded of the texturelike quality of life as she
compares life to a passage through a series of layers of experiences (55).
    The central issue that this chapter ("Achilles, O Achilles") addresses
is death—how one prepares for it, meets it, and whether the safe life
is preferable to a more dangerous one, like a flyer's. The chapter addresses the tragedy associated with the current war, but it also introduces the primary conflict of the story, Eve's struggle to accommodate
the hazards of life intellectually and emotionally, and it provides the
link between the threat of death that faces men during war, or when
involved in any hazardous activity, and the anxieties that women can
experience as well. Lindbergh establishes a spectrum of courage with
men in combat at one end, and women in their daily lives at the other
end. In the middle of this spectrum are pilots like Gerald (and here
Lindbergh seems to be reminding her readers of her husband's courage,
a quality that might have been questioned as a result of his recent

noninterventionist activities), and women like Eve, who occasionally find themselves caught up in hazardous activities.

The next landmark over which they fly is the Reims cathedral, and while it is linked to other World-War-I battlefield locations—the Marne, Verdun, the Argonne—it also establishes a link to another important aspect of Eve's intellectual struggle, the spiritual mode, which is directly tied to her strong belief in life. Eve concludes that, much as she objects to the discomforts of flying, she values it because it creates an intense feeling of life. She soon finds her carefully reasoned conclusions severely tested when they become lost in cloud and fog after they cross the Alps.

The clouds thicken around them as they enter the airspace over Switzerland, and even though Eve can see some glimpses of the countryside below—Neuchatel, a corner of Lake Geneva—her view of the earth beneath becomes more and more limited by cloud. Finally, they enter the Alps, and the breathtaking sight of the bright snow-clad mountain peaks towering above them causes Eve to question briefly the capability of their frail craft to carry them safely. The Alps represent a world of extra-human activity; Eve compares them to "giants," past which she and Gerald are moving cautiously (72).

Once past the highest part of the Alps Eve and Gerald suddenly find themselves surrounded by clouds; chapter 7, "The Anteroom," describes their futile efforts to find a clear area and to discover their exact position. As they attempt to find a break in the clouds through which they hope to descend and fly to their destination, Eve notices how the cloud layers have begun to look like layers of cloth, each with its own special texture. Once Gerald finally decides upon a course of action, however, Eve's fear begins to decrease; as Gerald begins a controlled descent into the clouds beneath them, Eve finds strength in small tasks. She realizes that their descent could well end in their deaths, if they fly into trees or a hilltop. Yet she is now prepared to face that threat, for she realizes that fear occurs when one is waiting to face death; when one is actually in the process of facing death, as they are in their descent, fear fades (106–7).

As they continue their descent through the clouds, Eve attempts to discover what it is that is helping her to overcome her fear of death. She realizes that in the act of accepting death her sense of fear is dissipated and she feels a "strange ecstasy": "This then was life:—not to be hurried, not to be afraid, not to be imprisoned in oneself. To be open, aware, vulnerable—even to fear, even to pain, even to death. Then only did one feel ecstasy filling one up to the brim" (111).

At the moment Eve gains this insight the aircraft descends below the level of the clouds, and she can tell from observing Gerald's reaction that they have safely escaped from danger. In the minutes before the aircraft lands Eve considers that she has been too apprehensive in the past because she has "hoarded," or protected, her gift of life instead of accepting the things that threaten it: loss, danger, the urgency of the passage of time (118). As she accommodates herself to the idea of accepting the existence of forces that threaten life, she feels as if she has experienced a kind of rebirth, in herself, and in the child she is carrying.

The Steep Ascent is an accurate account of a frightening experience in the course of what should have been a routine flight from England to Italy. But if that were its only point, Lindbergh could more easily have told that story in the first-person, narrative style of *North to the Orient* and *Listen! the Wind* and without quite so much of the philosophical meditation with which the story is perhaps too heavily invested. Rather, the story is Lindbergh's translation of a personal incident into a parable of universal experience for all women. And, more than this, it is also part religious testament and part apologia for recently concluded activities in her own life, aspects which are addressed in the preface.

The preface to *The Steep Ascent* contains an explanation about why the story is so obviously personal experience related in thinly disguised fictional form:

For this story is fiction and not biography. Or, to be more accurate, it is a fictional account of an actual incident. It is not primarily an adventure story, at least certainly not one of physical adventure. And only in the most accidental and superficial sense can it even be called a flying story. Fundamentally it is simply a woman's story, the story of a woman's life and ordeal—any woman and any ordeal. (vi)

That Lindbergh intended the story to describe everywoman's ordeal is evident in a letter to her friend Sue Vaillant on 17 March 1943, in which she wrote that

I have put everything in it—everything I learned from that life in the past. It is a flight over the Alps but it could be anything. Childbirth or getting married, or the mental and moral struggles one has. There are those same peaks ("Is this all there is to the Alps?") and those same abysses ("I am abandoned—they have abandoned me!"). It is my whole life. (*WW*, 331)

The narrative speaks to women in a number of ways: most obviously, the narrator is a woman, and the reactions of the narrator to the in-flight experiences are described in language of activities and everyday objects familiar to women, including household items, food, and clothing. Eve's duties and responsibilities on the flight are typical of a woman less familiar with flying activities than an experienced flier like Anne Lindbergh; although it is evident that Eve has flown with Gerald before, she seems less comfortable in and less accustomed to the flying environment. The intent to address the story to a large audience of women is also evident in the narrator's name: *Eve*, after the first and most universal of women; and *Alcott*, probably after Louisa May Alcott, one of Lindbergh's favorite authors of children's stories, whose most familiar theme was appropriate behavior for young ladies. In addition, Eve is pregnant, and her pregnancy serves as an all-encompassing sym-bol of a kind of physical death and renewal specifically applicable to women. An equally important symbolic device in the story, that of *texture*, combines elements of nature and daily life in an appropriately domestic image suggesting the safety and protection afforded by a va-riety of appropriately interwoven threads.

   The story serves as a symbolic statement of a different kind of moral and mental struggle that Lindbergh had experienced lately, one that had little to do with flying—her noninterventionist writings and the public reaction to them. It is clear in her diary entries of the period that her struggle to write her three nonintervention essays was an ar-duous one, a struggle that left her often unsatisfied with the results, largely because a part of her was in strong sympathy with the Allied anti-German effort. As she notes in a diary entry for 23 February 1943, made while she was writing *The Steep Ascent*: "I have had three big things to fight against in my life. The first was just sorrow (the Case [of the murder of the Lindbergh baby]), the second was fear (the flights), and the third is bitterness (this whole war struggle). And the third is the hardest" (*WW*, 328). The bitterness resulted from attacks against her and her husband for their stands on American noninterven-tion, but there was a kind of artistic dissatisfaction, too, for she deeply admired the personal participation in the war and the resulting literary efforts of Antoine de Saint-Exupéry.

   Saint-Exupéry had returned to France immediately after meeting the Lindberghs to volunteer for military service. Refusing a staff as-signment, he was able to find a flying position with a French recon-naissance unit. He miraculously escaped death during a number of hazardous missions before and during the invasion of France. After France fell in June 1940, he eventually made his way to the United States, where he wrote *Flight to Arras*, a fictionalized account of his reconnaissance flying, published in 1942. Lindbergh was especially impressed with *Flight to Arras*, which she read in the winter of 1942, while she was working on *The Steep Ascent*, because its primary narrative device was an extended reconnaissance flight over the French countryside during the German invasion. During the course of the flight the narrator, who is Saint-Exupéry himself, passes from anger at the war and rejection of his participation in the war to a condition of understanding and acceptance at the end of the flight. The narrator's flight is a moral as well as a physical rite of passage during which he recognizes and accepts the essential value of the French people and the French culture and his relationship to them. The intent of the book was clearly to prescribe a patient and understanding view of the strife in France.

The Steep Ascent depicts a similar kind of intellectual progress across a moral landscape. But Eve Alcott is flying not in a wartime but a peacetime sky, and the allegorical meaning is of a broader nature. Eve departs from a safe, familiar environment and flies toward a more hazardous, unfamiliar destination. As she and her husband proceed along their chosen route, they pass over visual landmarks that represent various aspects of forces and institutions that affect daily living: the house where they are living (family relationships), the Channel (separation), the battlefields (war and strife), the Reims cathedral (religious and spiritual belief), the Alps (supreme physical and intellectual achievement), and finally the fog- and cloud-filled air (of personal and moral confusion). The escape from confusion is represented in the blind spiral descent, which is a kind of intellectual death and rebirth. As Lindbergh admitted, the flight in *The Steep Ascent* symbolized her "whole life," her marriage, the birth of her children, her search for creativity and family stability.

When *The Steep Ascent* was published, Lindbergh was saddened by but not totally surprised to learn of the public resistance to its appearance. The Book-of-the-Month Club declined to make it available to its readers and the *Reader's Digest* also turned it down, primarily for reasons of negative reader reaction (*WW*, 408). Harcourt, Brace issued a first edition of 25,000 copies early in March 1944. Later, however, after most reviewers received it favorably (*WW*, 419, 422), the book was reprinted.

The one reader whose reaction Lindbergh most cared about was Saint-Exupéry. When she learned early in August 1944 that he had been reported missing in action on a P-38 reconnaissance flight over southern France on 31 July, she was profoundly shocked and saddened. In an extended diary entry for 8 October she writes of many things, of Charles's return from the war in the Pacific, of their new house in Connecticut, and of the passing of Saint-Exupéry: "And my last book [*The Steep Ascent*], which had gone out like a letter to him and never reached him, of what use was that? No one could really understand it, not as he could have." (*WW*, 447).

The flight in *The Steep Ascent* is more an internal than an external event; it is more intellectual than physical. In Lindbergh's three flying books the flights described in each grow shorter, but the experiences of those flights, and the meanings those experiences suggest, are described in greater detail. The movement from external description to internal reflection is evident, and it marks the path that Lindbergh's subsequent writings will follow; external description will serve primarily as prologue to internal meditation.

Chapter Eight
Postwar Essays

The spiritual aspect of Lindbergh's thought that is first seen in *The Wave of the Future* and that is an integral part of *The Steep Ascent* is also evident in five postwar essays she wrote from 1947 through 1950. Her personal concern with the hardships of life in postwar Europe, especially in those countries she visited most often before the war—England, France, Germany—is combined with an emphasis on spiritual qualities. The meditational, reasoned style blends with a message of international cooperation. Although these essays were never anthologized after their initial publication in American periodicals, they illustrate an important phase of her literary career, representing an important transitional step in Lindbergh's philosophy and work, and they merit consideration in this study.

After the end of the war the Lindberghs settled into a reasonably normal living routine, perhaps for the first time in their lives. Although Charles Lindbergh continued to be active in his aviation consulting work, their permanent home in Connecticut provided them and their children the security and stability they had sought for fifteen years. In addition, both Lindberghs were essentially reestablished in the good graces of the American public, Charles through his participation in the war was a test pilot, and Anne through the favorable reception to *The Steep Ascent*. In addition, she had seen two book reviews published; these book reviews had provided an opportunity to discuss meaningful but less controversial philosophical ideas than those of *The Wave of the Future*.

In the summer of 1947 Lindbergh traveled to Europe. Her visit to postwar Europe was prompted by her concern about old friends and by a strong desire to see for herself the damage that had been suffered by the European cities. Much of her creative energy from 1947 to 1950 was devoted to the assessment and description of her European travel experiences. The result of this effort was a series of five articles, published in 1948 and 1950, that can be collectively thought of as an extended impression of postwar Europe. The five articles, in order of publication, are:

"The Flame of Europe," *Reader's Digest,* 52 January 1948, 141–46

"One Starts at Zero," *Reader's Digest,* 52 February 1948, 73–75

"Anywhere in Europe," *Harper's Magazine,* 196 April 1948, 300–302

"Airliner to Europe," *Harper's Magazine,* 197 September 1948, 43–47

"Our Lady of Risk," *Life,* 29 July 1950, 80–91

"Airliner to Europe" describes Lindbergh's experiences as she travels to Europe by commercial airliner. The essay establishes three primary themes, themes common to the other essays as well. The first theme is one of contrast in values, in which the Old World (Europe) is contrasted to the new (America), and older cultures are contrasted to modern life. The second theme is one of dislocation, of the difficulty of seeing one's environment clearly, of the difficulty of feeling at home in a foreign land, of the difficulty of communicating one's feelings to others. The third theme is the necessity of spiritual values, of which the church is the central symbol and image.

The contrast of old and new is evident when Lindbergh discovers that their old North Beach seaplane base, in Flushing, New York, has become La Guardia Field, a large and impersonal transportation facility. A porter carries her bags into a modern air terminal where soft-drink dispensers and candy-bar machines line the walls. She unfavorably compares modern air travel to the mode of flying she knew before the war:

Aviation belonged to the air then, and you were in the air. Now you go into a closed rotunda, and scuttle down a subway passage with crowds of other passengers. A few seconds' dash in the sunshine to the boarding ramp (rolled up like some piece of medieval war-machinery), and up the steps into that dark pullman car of a plane. Soft carpets, upholstered armchairs, curtains, and only a little round peephole of a window from which to look out at the sky— the whole sky! Flying has shut out the sky. ("Airliner to Europe," 43–44)

She finds it difficult to accustom herself to the almost excessive comfort of modern air travel; she misses the noise, the wind, the temperature variations. She is unable to appreciate fully the pleasures of modern travel because she cannot really experience the sensations of travel; she cannot *feel* what it is like to fly: "One is enclosed in a vacuum with no sense of the element one is passing through" (45).

When their arriving plane passes over the French countryside en route to Paris, Lindbergh is pleased to see that the church occupies the central position in the towns and villages. She especially appreciates the fact that open spaces around the churches provide an appropriate perspective: "To me," she comments, "the space also indicates a respectful distance, a reverent drawing back, a dropping to one's knees before something sacred" (46).

As they arrive at Le Bourget, she thinks of herself as an outsider, "a stranger who has made a swift and easy passage from the new world to the old, but [who is] not fooled by the ease of passage into thinking the two worlds are one" (47). Technological advances, she argues, are not in themselves the key to communication. The necessary tool for bridging the gap of national and cultural differences is common experience, derived from shared sufferings, hopes, and beliefs. Her final observation, like her opening comment, presents a contrast; in this case, instead of the old in opposition to the new, the human element is set in contrast to technological development: "An airplane, like a horse, can't make friends for a man; it can only carry him closer to his friends. The miracle of communication—and I still believe it is the greatest miracle in life—is not in the machine but in the man" (47).

The essay establishes many continuities with her previous writing: recognition of the role of the aircraft in expanding awareness of the human community, demonstration of the importance of perception and the value of space, and acknowledgment of the centrality of religious belief. Through contrasts of old and new, technology and human experience, and alienation and community, a tension is created that subsequent essays amplify and resolve.

"Anywhere in Europe" is a prose tone poem, a Kafka-esque study of postwar European bureaucracy. The essay paints the bleakest picture of European conditions of any of the five essays written at this time. It describes the sensations applicants for goods or services would experience as they moved through a typical bureaucratic edifice, often an old mansion, stripped of its former trappings, "but still redolent of the elegance of another day" ("Anywhere in Europe," 300). Applicants are given forms to fill out, forms on which the requested information may be difficult for Europeans to supply, because their residences and their occupations may not be fixed; the war has caused a good deal of turmoil in European business and family life. Americans living in Europe may have no difficulty in providing the necessary information, but they must submit to the slow, mind-numbing application process.

From behind one of the doors marked "Absolutely forbidden to enter" appears a young American soldier, who has apparently been able to obtain his desired service. His success with the monolithic bureaucracy gives hope to the others. As the American departs, the spirit of the small community of applicants lifts noticeably, and Lindbergh wonders if this feeling—"expectancy, a possibility of belief, an early March forerunner of hope" (302)—is what we have to offer Europe.

"The Flame of Europe," the earliest published essay of the group, is also the most complex and the most comprehensive. It occupies the central, or keystone, position in these postwar essays because it moves from a summary of the unhappy conditions in Europe toward a positive and persuasive statement of the kinds of commitment and action Lindbergh believes will be required of her American readers. She opens the essay with the statement that she traveled to Europe to talk to individuals and to gather information about conditions there. After her two-month visit, however, she was faced with the realization that "it is almost impossible to look at Europe in terms of separate details, separate individuals, or even separate nations. All of Europe reduces itself to one bleak stark picture. Europe is hungry—for food, for material, for hope" ("The Flame of Europe," 141).

These three items—food, material, hope—represent the central issues of the essay. France needs bread, England lacks meat, and Germany faces famine conditions. Even though Germany is a conquered country and France and England the victors, the differences in their conditions are, according to Lindbergh, "in degree more than in kind." "And," she adds, "all differences are gradually being leveled in the sinking standard of living of all Europe" (142). She sees conditions in France and England and Germany not merely as the result of six years of war, but as the effects of the decay of an entire civilization: "This house, with its roof on the ground, its interior despoiled, its foundations crumbling—this house is a symbol. The basic values of our civilization are crumbling away like this rubble" (143).

Lindbergh had given her views on the decay of civilization earlier, in *The Wave of the Future,* in which she stated her fears over the effects of the "decay, weakness and blindness" in the attitudes of modern democracies (*WF,* 33–34); these ideas were continued in her 1941 essay, "Reaffirmation," in which she expressed anxiety about "the impact of science on the delicately balanced life of man" ("Reaffirmation," 683). Her reiteration of these fears in 1948 illustrates the extent of her belief and the consistency of her themes.

Comparing the condition of Europe to a candle whose flame is on the verge of extinction for lack of wax to feed the flame, Lindbergh exhorts her American readers not to ignore the situation in Europe. She reminds them that American weapons as well as European helped to create the destruction that occurred during the war, and she argues that European civilization and American civilization are inextricably linked: "The flame that is burning in Europe is the flame of our civilization, our culture, our basic beliefs" (144).

The essay illustrates the pattern of contrast, tension, and resolution as the individual is matched against the group, security against freedom, and science against religion. Lindbergh does not suggest that one of the two is preferable to the other; her purpose is to show that there is a conflict, a tension between the two, and to suggest the way in which the opposing forces can be accommodated. The fundamental oppositions of the essay, however, are presented in the contrast of prewar European conditions to postwar conditions, and in the resulting change necessary in American attitudes to recognize and to improve the European situation. The ideas in this essay follow logically from those she described in her noninterventionist essays of 1939 and 1940. She concludes the essay on a strongly religious note, reminding her readers of the original meaning of the current Christmas season, linking the miracle of the first Christmas with the miracle Europe will need in order to recover fully. The spiritual aspect of her thought becomes increasingly important in the last two essays of the postwar group.

The pattern of the possibility of the resolution of the opposing conditions described in the previous essays is outlined in the final two essays of the period, "One Starts at Zero" and "Our Lady of Risk." In both Lindbergh focuses specifically on the postwar rebuilding efforts of three small French communities. The shorter and earlier essay of the two, "One Starts at Zero," describes her visits to the towns of Vire and Saint Lô and the rebuilding efforts she observed there.

The mayor of Vire uses the phrase "one starts at zero" to indicate how the members of his community must begin their rebuilding efforts. Lindbergh builds on the mayor's account of the appearance of the city before it was leveled by Allied bombers to establish a contrast between the beauty of the past and the destruction of the present. The postwar remnants of centuries of human labor include "a desert of empty lots," "gaping cellars, loose foundation blocks, pulverized stone" ("One Starts at Zero," 73). The mayor proudly shows Lindbergh how the townspeople are attempting to rebuild the school and business establishments. But she also notes that rationing of food and tobacco still exists three years after the war, and some families are living in bombed-out buildings. In Saint-Lô Lindbergh is directed to a hill in the center of town that contains the ruin of the village church. Here she finds a few men involved in the nearly impossible task of restoring the building.

The essay contrasts the ruined conditions of the French villages with the indestructible spirit of the villagers themselves. Ironically, the damage that Lindbergh observes is the result of Allied bombings. Although never explicitly pointed out, the damage caused by the liberation effort is evident. In addition to the contrast of Allied destruction and French indestructibility, the essay examines the theme of the outsider and the problem of perception. After admitting to the mayor of Vire that she cannot imagine what the town must have been like before the war, Lindbergh says that "the stranger sees only with the physical eye, not with the eye of memory" (74). In this essay, as in every other in the group, Lindbergh draws attention to an appropriate framework of perception, to the crucial importance of sympathetic understanding of Europeans and their environment through a cultural vision that sees the present in the context of the past.

She emphasizes spiritual values, concluding her account with the description of the ruined church at Saint-Lô. The ruined church serves as a symbol of the reconstructed attitudes Americans need to bring with them to a true understanding of the needs and mood of postwar Europe. The church as a symbol of enduring cultural values occupies the central position of her final essay of the period, "Our Lady of Risk."

"Our Lady of Risk" appeared in the July 1950 issue of *Life Magazine*, following Lindbergh's second postwar trip to Europe. The essay features an interview with Dom Alexis, the founder and head of the reconstructed twelfth-century Cistercian Abbey of Boquen in Brittany, an institution Lindbergh had first heard of during their residence at Illiec in 1938. Dom Alexis had come to the abbey in 1936, after it had been abandoned for over a hundred years; he initiated a series of repairs to the structure and gradually drew other people to share his life of rebuilding and religious contemplation. Although the essay is primarily about the abbey and its founder, it incorporates much of the information she obtained during her travels across Europe, and the abbey itself emerges as a symbol of the new order for which Lindbergh sees the Europeans searching. Our Lady of Risk is a statute of a stone madonna carved by one of the brothers in the abbey; the name was derived from a New Testament passage. The statue represents the spirit of the postwar brotherhood in which the losses of the war give birth to new life and renewed spirit.

In the second half of the essay Lindbergh considers the abbey's significance as a symbolic institution in the modern world, one whose purpose reflects the goals and needs of postwar Europeans. She characterizes the abbey as the kind of habitat in which the old ideal of balancing thought and action can be made meaningful in a modern world. Dom Alexis represents someone who has successfully blended the two aspects of action and contemplation, work and prayer.

The essay reflects Lindbergh's sincere belief in and commitment to the idea of spiritual rejuvenation. Its conclusion features a remark of Dom Alexis with which Lindbergh is clearly in agreement: "'In Boquen,' as he once wrote, 'one sails on the full tide of faith'" ("Our Lady of Risk," 91). The "wave of the future" and the "full tide of faith" seem evidently to result from similar currents in Lindbergh's symbolic sea, whose metaphoric significance will soon achieve its greatest form in *Gift from the Sea*.

Chapter Nine
Gift from the Sea

Lindbergh's first major postwar publication—*Gift from the Sea*—is deservedly her best-known and most popular work. This series of essays, meditations on a variety of seashells, characterizes the concerns of American women, although it is also for and about men. The central symbols of the book are seashells, which represent different aspects of personal and social relationships; the shells provide a natural metaphor for illuminating and clarifying a complex topic. These essays reveal Lindbergh at her stylistic and thematic best, linking physical description to meditative insight. The essays address the definition of self and the development of meaningful relationships with others.

Gift from the Sea resulted from Lindbergh's need to resolve her own mental conflicts and not from any idea of assessing the issues perplexing the American woman in general. "I began these pages for myself," she says in the opening sentence of the introduction, "in order to think out my own particular pattern of living, my own individual balance of life, work and human relationships" (*GS,* 9). Although it was finally prompted by a number of family events that occurred in the early 1950s, her need to clarify her own role as the wife of Charles Lindbergh, as a mother, and as a woman with creative aspirations began soon after her marriage to the famous aviator.

As her career as a writer began to take shape, she pondered the special pressures that women face in their attempts to define themselves as individuals. In a letter to her cousin Mary Scandrett written in January 1937, she provides a detailed account of her meditations on women's activities and purposes: "Isn't it possible for a woman to be a woman and yet produce something tangible besides children, something that stands up in a man's world? In other words, is it possible to live up to women's standards and men's standards at the same time? Is it possible to make them the same? (As the feminists do.)" (*FN,* 124). Lindbergh admitted that she did not prefer to make the attempt because "it involves sacrificing things I am not prepared to sacrifice":

> For a lot of women do succeed in combining the two. But I think they do it (if successfully) at the price of a pigeonholed life—a man's life. Because in order to compete with men they must concentrate their energies into a narrow line. And I think in doing that they deny themselves the special attributes and qualities of women.
> I don't think women should try to be straight lines. I think they should be circles. (*FN*, 124)

In 1941 she notes in her diary that she is working on a "feminist essay," adding that "the problem of the woman and her 'work' is still so unsolved" (*WW*, 170). Later that year she records the fact that she is doing some "rather uninspired" work on an essay she calls "Women and a Career," but she says nothing about its content (*WW*, 237).

After the war Charles's consulting work continued, and she found that her five growing children placed increasing demands on her time. In 1950 their ages ranged from eighteen to five, the three boys older and the two girls younger. According to comments she made to Julie Nixon Eisenhower, the years after the war were "the most difficult of their marriage" (Eisenhower, *Special People*, 140). Charles Lindbergh, a man of phenomenal energy, directed much of that energy toward activities outside the family, primarily his aviation consulting work, often leaving Anne alone. "It was not easy when he was gone," she said; "in those years I was learning to be a person on my own" (141). Adding to her sense of aloneness were the deaths of two important family members: first her mother-in-law, Mrs. Evangeline Lindbergh, who passed away in the fall of 1954, and then her own mother, Mrs. Elizabeth Morrow, who died early in 1955.

The event that most directly helped to bring about the writing of *Gift from the Sea* was a visit that Lindbergh made to the South Atlantic coast of the United States in the company of her younger sister, Constance, in the spring of 1955. The change brought on by their temporary escape from the duties of the home combined with the pleasure of living at the warm seaside linked the external world of the sea and the internal world of personal reflection. The focal point of communication between the two worlds was provided by a series of five small seashells or shell-like structures, each one signifying a separate aspect of spiritual or social issues.

Four Shells

Gift from the Sea is a brief book, 128 pages long, consisting of eight essays that describe the narrator's physical progress toward the sea, along the shore, and away from the sea, simultaneously charting her intellectual engagement with the subjects of womanhood and women's relationships. The first and the last of the essays depict movement toward and away from the beach, while the central six essays focus upon individual shell structures and their symbolic relation to aspects of women's personal relationships.

"The Beach," the short opening essay, describes the special atmosphere of the seashore—the heat, the moist air, the movement of the sand—where bodily fatigue brings mental relaxation and where "one is forced against one's mind, against all tidy resolutions, back into the primeval rhythms of the sea-shore" (*GS,* 16). Lindbergh establishes a mood in which the natural motion of the sea disengages the mind from its mechanical, ordered habit of daily living and enables it to discover submerged treasures of its lower layers so that individual ideas will appear of their own accord, like shells discovered on a beach, true "gifts from the sea."

The first shell that Lindbergh examines is the channeled whelk, a small, curved, finger-size shell; its name provides the title of the second essay. The shell first housed the whelk, a snail-like creature; then it housed a tiny hermit crab, whose tracks Lindbergh sees "like a delicate vine on the sand" (21). The shell represents outer protection, a covering over one's life, the external qualities of the self. She admires the simple perfection of the shell:

Its shape, swelling like a pear in the center, winds in a gentle spiral to the pointed apex. Its color, dull gold, is whitened by a wash of salt from the sea. Each whorl, each faint knob, each criss-cross vein in its egg-shell texture, is as clearly defined as on the day of creation. ("The Channeled Whelk," 22).

The external pattern of her own life, however, is "blurred with moss, knobby with barnacles" (22). Lindbergh indicates a desire to *simplify* her life, to replace the fragmentation of her pattern of life caused by numerous daily activities with a sense of wholeness and coherence. She says that she wants to be "at peace" with herself, to discover a "singleness of eye, a purity of intention, a central core," to live "in Grace" (23).

The challenge facing the American woman is the challenge of managing endless family and social tasks and responsibilities: "This is not the life of simplicity but the life of multiplicity that the wise men warn us of. It leads not to unification but to fragmentation. It does not bring grace; it destroys the soul." (26–27). Lindbergh suggests that while the tendency toward fragmentation of one's life has probably always been present and can affect men as well as women, "the problem is particularly and essentially woman's" because a woman has "interests and duties, raying out in all directions from the central mother-core, like spokes from the hub of a wheel" (28). She develops the central metaphor of her concept of woman, the structured circle: "The pattern of our lives is essentially circular. We must be open to all points of the compass; husband, children, friends, home, community; stretched out, exposed, sensitive like a spider's web to each breeze that blows, to each call that comes" (28). The central conflict indicated here and throughout the book is one of centeredness opposed to distraction. The problem confronting the American woman, she says, is "how to remain whole in the midst of the distractions of life" (29).

Lindbergh concludes the essay by returning her focus from the inner world of personal meditation to the external world of the sea: "I am looking at the outside of a shell, the outside of my life—the shell. . . . The final answer, I know, is always inside. But the outside can give a clue, can help one to find the inside answer" (35). This essay establishes the pattern in the structure, theme, and mood for those to follow: the writer is less interested in biological aspects of seashells than their typological aspects. Each shell becomes a unique mirror for the observer, reflecting those mental images suggested by the physical characteristics of the shell and the intellectual perspective of the observer. The shell becomes transformed into a symbolic looking glass.

The third essay, "Moon Shell," is the pivotal essay in the book, for it marks a shift from the consideration of external aspects of the shell to internal aspects. In this essay personal assessment is the focus of analysis. The representative shell for this essay is the moon shell, the tightly wound snail shell:

On its smooth symmetrical face is pencilled with precision a perfect spiral, winding inward to the pinpoint center of the shell, the tiny dark core of the apex, the pupil of the eye. It stares at me, this mysterious single eye—and I stare back.

Now it is the moon, solitary in the sky, full and round, replete with power. Now it is the eye of a cat that brushes noiselessly through long grass at night. Now it is an island, set in ever-widening circles of waves, alone, self-contained, serene. (39–40)

Lindbergh links the shell with images rich in symbolic significance: the moon, an eye, an island. These images are separate yet interrelated: the moon represents the natural forces of woman, the eye suggests perception, and the island is a self-contained world. These three concepts become an important part of her analysis of the inner self, sharing qualities of mystery and centeredness. The island image links the narrator's physical environment to her intellectual exploration; it represents a sense of isolation in space and time and enables one to live "like a child or a saint in the immediacy of here and now" (40). The island image serves as the transition from contemplation of the shell to contemplation of the individual condition, as the essay begins with a meditation on the meaning of aloneness.

Lindbergh opposes the usual notion that it is neither desirable nor healthful to be alone; she argues that occasional isolation helps one to rediscover a sense of self, and that "we must re-learn to be alone" (42). The condition of aloneness, especially on a beach, puts one in closer touch with nature. As a result of her aloneness, she says, she finds herself in "harmony" with the "beauty of earth and air and sea" (43). Refreshed by the sense of fulfillment obtained through her solitary communion with nature, she wishes that nothing would occur to rob her of her sense of fulfillment—to diminish her store of self. This thought reminds her of woman's eternal conflict of self opposed to selflessness; "all her instinct as a woman," she says, "demands that she give" (45). That conditioned part of woman, Lindbergh argues, urges her to give naturally of herself, while the private part of the self resists the unselective giving urge. Lindbergh suggests that "what woman resents is not so much giving herself in pieces as giving herself purposelessly" (46).

Solitude, she suggests, can provide the key to discovering purposeful activity—not the condition of solitude itself, necessarily, but the insights that solitude can help to identify. The fundamental idea of her essay is that everyone, but especially women, should work toward establishing periodic moments of solitude. Lindbergh realizes that such an idea might appear to be "revolutionary" or "impossible," but she is thoroughly convinced of its necessity (48). Even mothers and housewives ("the great vacationless class") should schedule time to be alone (49). Time spent alone, Lindbergh says, is necessary for women "to find again the true essence of themselves: that firm strand which will be the indispensable center of a whole web of human relationships" (50). The image of a web at the center of human, family activities becomes transposed into the image of a wheel: "This is an end toward which we could strive—to be the still axis within the revolving wheel of relationships, obligations, and activities" (51).

Lindbergh continues her examination of the importance of the search for solitude with a discussion of the church as a traditional centering force and as a means for achieving spiritual wholeness (53–54). She concludes by suggesting that one's pursuit of centeredness could be seen as "revolutionary" because "almost every trend and pressure, every voice from the outside is against this new way of inward living" (57). Woman must be the "pioneer in this turning inward for strength," a task she is naturally suited for because she has traditionally lived a life of inner-directed activities (57).

The three images of moon, eye, and island are closely interrelated in the essay. The island represents the self-contained world, made perfect by its own completeness and self-sufficiency. The moon operates according to its own natural law and is uniquely representative of the feminine psyche. The eye is the core of perceptivity, which sees the wholeness of the island, understands the significance of the moon, and values the relationship between the two. All three share the characteristic of the perfection of the circle, at whose center woman is located, the hub of essential human activity.

The next essay, "Double-Sunrise," moves from consideration of the self to the intimate relationship, in which the self establishes a personal and meaningful relationship with a friend, the other. The double-sunrise shell, perfectly matched halves of a bivalve shell, symbolizes this shared relationship. More particularly, it represents the special bonding that occurs early in the relationship, when it is in its purest stage, before it is "weighed down with irrelevancies" (64). The sunrise pattern of the shell denotes this initial bonding—the relationship in the early morning of its life, prior to familiarity and the routine of daily living.

In Lindbergh's view the shared relationship can exist with any important member of the family—friend, lover, spouse, child. The special magic of the relationship is the sensation one experiences in making initial contact with the other individual. The essay is not, however, primarily about the qualities of that early relationship; its focus is directed toward the sense of loss as it disappears and the often wasteful attempt to recapture glimpses of that relationship after its newness has faded. The social and familial responsibilities of marriage, of raising children, and the pressures of domestic life and professional life can combine to tarnish the luster of the early relationship. This change is sad but inevitable and should be accepted with patience and understanding. As time passes, the man transfers the energy formerly devoted to the relationship into his work, while the woman transfers her energy into the development of other relationships, especially with each child in its infancy.

Nestled inside the body of the essay is the kernel of the idea with which she is most preoccupied throughout the essay, one which will be treated in greater length in "Argonauta." That idea is that the most beneficial alternate to the lost glow of the early relationship is self-discovery from within; no other individual can offer one the fulfillment one can find in oneself. True fulfillment comes from gaining self-knowledge, from understanding one's "true identity." One's true identity "is found in creative activity springing from within. It is found, paradoxically, when one loses oneself. One must lose one's life to find it. Woman can best refind herself by losing herself in some kind of creative activity of her own" (69).

The next essay takes as its central symbol the oyster shell, which represents the middle years of marriage. The oyster shell appropriately represents the later relationship because it is "fitted and formed by its own life and struggle to survive," and it is usually found "with small shells clinging to its humped back" (80). Its uneven shape reflects the additions and modifications that marriage, work, and children bring to the relationship and the figurative structure that houses it. The oyster's encrustations represent the daily record of a relationship that endures.

Lindbergh incorporates Saint-Exupéry's comment about love's consisting not of two people looking at each other, but looking outward in the same direction, to characterize the ideal condition of the marriage in its middle years (81). She blends Saint-Exupéry's statement with the image of the web: "The web of marriage is made by propinquity, in the day to day living side by side, looking outward and working outward in the same direction. It is woven in space and in time of the substance of life itself" (82). The oyster shell is an appropriate image of a relationship in its later stage because it is "humble," "awkward," and "ugly" (83). It lacks the perfect symmetry of the relationship in its early stages (the double-sunrise shell), and its lack of symmetry indicates a relationship that has changed from the envisioned life to the lived life.

But once again Lindbergh reveals her discomfort at tying her account of the self and the other too closely to a fixed system of symbols represented by the shells she finds along the beach; at this point in personal development, she says, she is "not sure that one has not grown too big for any shell at all" (84). And she suggests that in middle age one might be able to shed shells altogether, including the shells of ambition, of material accumulations and possessions, and the ego (84). One may outgrow even the oyster shell (88).

"The Argonauta"

The essays on the first four shells in *Gift from the Sea* present a well-balanced, ordered structure and unified thematic development. The movement from outer to inner qualities, then from private to public, reflects the imaginative movement of the narrator's mind as she turns from the external considerations of the shell to the internal arrangement of her own thoughts, thoughts suggested by the shell's appearance and her perceived interpretation of its meaning.

At this point a shift in the narrative approach occurs. The narrator abandons the practice of considering inert shells as the foci, or centers, of aspects of the shell, as she takes as the primary image of the next essay a form of sea life that differs significantly from the objects she has been examining. This shift occurs in the sixth essay, "Argonauta." The imaginative movement away from seashells as the thematic centers actually begins toward the middle of the previous essay, when the narrator wonders if the period of middle age should not be one in which the self attempts to shed the protective shells of youth.

"Argonauta" seems not to be as easily accessible as the previous essays; it does not follow the previous developmental pattern of shell-image-reflection-thought of the previous essays. Of the eight essays in the book, it is the most personal and the most natural in its construction.

The topic of the essay is the nature of the relationship between two ideally realized individuals. Lindbergh describes the relationship in poetic terms, for the situation she envisions is one of aesthetic perfection. That this condition is not common is evident in her statement that the fragile structure of the argonaut is not to be found along the shores of her beach: "I am fascinated by this image of the argonaut, whose temporary dwelling I have seen only as the treasure of a specialist's collection" (91–92). The argonaut represents someone who, in the fullness of intellectual maturity, "has left its shell for the open seas" (92). The more familiar shells have been left behind; in contemplating the argonaut "we are adventuring in the chartless seas of imagination" (93). The relationship described in this essay is a "meeting of two whole, fully developed people as persons" (93).

The principal part of the essay attempts to define the concept of "fully developed people." A phrase of the German poet Rainer Maria Rilke provides the key concept: "A relation that is meant to be of one human being to another . . . consists in this, that two solitudes protect and touch and greet each other" (94). The notion of "two solitudes" summarizes the sense that the book repeatedly conveys, that qualities of differentness and aloneness are acceptable and necessary in mature individuals and mature relationships. Lindbergh was drawn to Rilke's ideas, especially those expressed in letters seven and eight of his *Letters to a Young Poet*; these contain the passages that most caught Lindbergh's attention, for she believed that Rilke

foresaw a great change in the relationships between men and women, which he hoped in the future would no longer follow the traditional patterns of submission and domination or of possession and competition. He described a state in which there would be space and freedom for growth, and in which each partner would be the means of releasing the other. (94)

Lindbergh suggests to her women readers that they cannot attain true individuality until they have learned how to stand independently, to avoid swinging between the "two opposite poles of dependence and competition, of Victorianism and Feminism" (96). Men also, she suggests, should learn to develop the more personal, inner-directed sides of their personalities. She returns to Rilke's writings to make the point that while complete sharing is an impossibility, a "wonderful living side by side" can develop if the partners "succeed in loving the distance between them which makes it possible for each to see the other whole and against a wide sky!" (98) (the passage is adapted from the eighth letter of *Letters to a Young Poet*).

Lindbergh provides two examples of relationships shared by "two solitudes," one based on real life and one of a poetic nature. The real-life example consists of a delightful four-page sketch of a day she shared on the beach with her younger sister, Constance (99–103). The imaginative example compares coexistence in shared lives to a dance in which the partners move naturally together in accordance with a shared rhythm rather than in traditional social dancing in which one partner leads and the other follows (103–108).

The essay concludes with a return to the image of the argonauta as a symbol of the complete individual who is able to move easily according to the natural movement of nature, the sea. Lindbergh emphasizes the idea that there can be no real permanency, not in any condition of life, and certainly not in any "perfect" relationship. She closes by emphasizing that the value of the relationship lies not in its length of time but in individual awareness of its importance:

Security in a relationship lies neither in looking back to what it was in nostalgia, nor forward to what it might be in dread or anticipation, but living in the present relationship and accepting it as it is now. For relationships, too, must be like islands. One must accept them for what they are here and now, within their limits—islands, surrounded and interrupted by the sea, continually visited and abandoned by the tides. One must accept the security of the wingèd life, of ebb and flow, of intermittency. (109)

After moving from consideration of the external aspects of the self, to the internal aspects, to the early shared relationship, to the later relationship, Lindbergh concludes her exploration of the self and personal relationships with a demonstration of the value of solitude or aloneness and of the necessary tentativeness of any relationship, early or late. Having constructed an intellectual examination based on the concrete symbols of four distinct and unique seashells, she closes by deemphasizing the importance she had placed on them: "And my shells? I can sweep them all into my pocket. They are only there to remind me that the sea recedes and returns eternally" (110).

The Concluding Essays

The two final essays continue the movement of closure initiated toward the end of the "Argonauta" essay. In the seventh essay, "A Few Shells," the narrator is preparing to leave the island in anticipation of her return to a more structured routine of daily living in urban Connecticut. In addition to marking a withdrawal from the beach, the essay also describes the process by which she selects the few truly significant shells she will keep out of the many she collected during her stay. Each shell will be valuable for the particular beauty it represents, beauty that would be overwhelmed in a large collection. The solitude that each shell includes—the space around it—will add to its beauty "for it is only framed in space that beauty blooms" (114).

The shells will also serve to remind her of the special set of values she has discovered while on the island—her "island-precepts": simplicity in living; balance in intellectual, spiritual, and physical activity; unrushed work habits; space; time for solitude and for sharing; closeness to nature (120). Lindbergh closes by acknowledging that her shells will serve as her "island eyes," her special way of seeing life.

The concluding essay, "The Beach at My Back," contrasts the central ideas of the book with the challenges of the complexities of modern life; Lindbergh suggests that the values she has been discussing—"the search for outward simplicity, for inner integrity, for fuller relationship"—can help in addressing the problems of modern life (123). She argues that America has been too much preoccupied with the future to enjoy the present satisfactorily, and that the special mode of seeing the world that women possess can be a positive contribution to providing a more balanced perspective in the world:

The here, the now, and the individual, have always been the special concern of the saint, the artist, the poet, and—from time immemorial—the woman. In the small circle of the home she has never quite forgotten the particular uniqueness of each member of the family; the spontaneity of now; the vividness of here. This is the basic substance of life. (127)

Compared to the more aggressive approach of feminist writings of the 1960s and 1970s, Lindbergh's style appears conservative, even traditional; it is characterized by a quiet, reasoning tone of confidence and strength. Even though she thinks that some of her ideas are "revolutionary" (57), her rhetoric, restrained by conditioning and experience, seems to speak the language of accommodation, of acceptance of a world in which women's roles are the traditional roles of spouse, mother, homemaker.

Lindbergh did acknowledge, in a postscript to *Gift from the Sea* added twenty years after its initial publication, "*Gift from the Sea* Reopened," that she had misspoken in two aspects of her discussion. The first was her assumption that "women's coming of age had been largely won by the Feminists of my mother's generation" (132), and she admitted that many victories in the area of women's rights remained to be won. The second aspect involved the omission of a final stage in the progress of a woman's life, the period that occurs after the children have left the home. Lindbergh referred to this stage as the time of "the abandoned shell," a period she had not reached when *Gift from the Sea* was first published. This stage is characterized by solitude, the commodity she wished for more of in earlier stages: "when a mother is left, the lone hub of a wheel, with no other lives revolving about her, she faces a total re-orientation. It takes time to re-find the center of gravity" (134).

Gift from the Sea combines the best features of Lindbergh's writing; its style is conversational, and the persuasiveness of her argument is assisted by the logical appeal of her symbolic seashells. Her outlook on the definition of the self and relationships with others contains a blend of practicality and idealism. The rhetorical approach of *The Wave of the Future*—a reasoning process with the reader—is brought to bear on a topic that is not weighted with the more volatile subject of the earlier book.

Lindbergh's voice remains the representative voice of those women who do not deny their traditional roles in their search for personal and professional fulfillment. Hers is not the voice of a woman who wants to stand alone, but of a woman who wants to stand on an equal basis with the partner of her choice. Lindbergh does not attempt to deny traditional values of womanhood, but to understand and accept those values and to build upon them.

Chapter Ten
The Unicorn and Other Poems

The Unicorn and Other Poems reveals Lindbergh's long-term interest in poetry, which, like other genres, she adapted to her primary goal of philosophical expression. The poems in this volume reveal a maturity of conception in their individual construction and in their thematic arrangement. Lindbergh is more interested in poems as vehicles for ideas than as models of individual poetic forms. Her poems achieve their greatest impact more as a result of their comprehensive significance than from their separate achievements. While a number of poems in the collection are in such recognizable forms as the ballad and sonnet, Lindbergh's most effective poetic form is unstructured, organically derived from the subject of the poem.

Poetry was an important part of Lindbergh's creative life; she read poetry in times of stress and leisure, and she frequently wrote poetry to document occasions of personal significance. Reading and writing poetry helped her to place crucial periods and events in her life in a meaningful perspective and to isolate the key emotions and achievements. She constantly read poetry, and she often noted passages of her favorite poems in her diaries and in her published works. Her diaries testify to the fact that she read extensively among the American, British, and Continental poets, including Robert Frost, W. B. Yeats, Hilda Doolittle, James Elroy Flecker, Ezra Pound, Rainer Maria Rilke, Edward Thomas, Coventry Patmore, John Masefield, and James Stephens. *North to the Orient* contains passages from the writings of Emily Dickinson and Japanese haiku; *Listen! the Wind* contains excerpts from the writings of Thomas Traherne, Humbert Wolfe, Henry King, and Elizabeth Madox Roberts. Poets represented in *Gift from the Sea* include W. H. Auden, John Donne, and William Blake. *The Steep Ascent* includes passages from T. S. Eliot and Patrick Shaw-Stewart; Edna St. Vincent Millay is quoted in *Dearly Beloved,* and T. S. Eliot, Eleanor Wylie, and Abbie Huston Evans are represented in *Earth Shine.*

Even during her aviation-related travels with her husband, she entertained herself with her reading; shortly after her marriage she notes in a letter to her mother that she is making it a practice to "learn a poem or two every afternoon resting after the day's flight" (*HG,* 118). She also writes that she reads poetry in the aircraft when the weather is cloudy. In later years she worked briefly on an "anthology of her favorite poems and prose quotations," which was to have been entitled *O to Whom* (*WW,* 129n). It was never published; a manuscript copy is located in the Smith College Library.

The Early Poems (1925–1935)

Stimulated by her literature and writing classes at Smith College, Lindbergh wrote numerous poems, essays, and stories, many of which were published in the college magazine. By the time she had graduated, in June 1928, three essays, two stories, and eight poems had appeared in the pages of the *Smith College Monthly.* The first published poem, "Caprice," appeared in October 1926; "Safe" and "Unicorn" both appeared in January 1927; "A Certain Woman" and "Letter with a Foreign Stamp" were published in February 1927; "To —" and "Magnolia Tree" came out in May 1927; and "Remembrance" was printed in June 1928.

After her engagement to Charles Lindbergh was announced, industrious reporters returned to Smith College, discovered the poems she had written, and republished a number of them, five of which appeared in 9 March and 16 March issues of the *Literary Digest*: "Caprice," "Unicorn," "A Certain Woman," "Letter with a Foreign Stamp," and "Remembrance." The *Literary Digest* commentary in its 9 March issue, which was devoted to an announcement of the Lindbergh-Morrow engagement, said that Anne Morrow had already "won her spurs as a poet."

The high percentage of poems written in her undergraduate days indicates that she was strongly drawn to poetry as a form of artistic expression. These early poems reveal a variety of styles and a high level of achievement. They also illuminate important aspects of her creative approach and personal philosophy.

The central poem of her Smith College period is "Unicorn," the poem that introduces the symbol of special personal and poetic significance. "Unicorn" combines the varied elements of her earlier poetry as it looks ahead to the images and ideas of her later poetry. In "Unicorn" we can discover the ingredients that are to be found in her later poetry and prose: colorful details, emotionally charged moods, echoes

of children's literature, the theme of flight and escape, and the inclusion of a natural setting:

Unicorn

Everything today has been
   "Heavy" and "Brown."
Bring me a Unicorn
   To ride about the town!

Bring me a Unicorn
   As little and as white
As the new moon
   On its first night.

Green orchids, to deck him,
   The De Bussy-shade
Like the green-gold eyes
   Of a mermaid.

Red pomegranates
   For him to eat
Or small purple plums
   Lush and sweet.

And I will kneel each morning
   To polish bright his hoofs
That they may gleam each moon-night
   We ride over roofs!

The unicorn, fed emotionally suggestive foods (red pomegranates, purple plums) and adorned with flowers of romance (green orchids), represents a means of emotional, spiritual, and physical escape. The
unicorn operates with total freedom, enabling its rider to achieve un-
common experiences and sensations possible only through flight. The
notion of flight as escape and as exceptional experience may well have
been inspired by aviation achievements of the day. Certainly the poem
is prophetic of Lindbergh's future activities, as the 9 March issue of the
Literary Digest observed, when it noted that she had "already shown a
certain amount of air-mindedness" in the poem.
  Over ten years elapsed before another poem appeared in an American
journal, but it was an event-filled decade for her: she married, gave
birth to three children, suffered the loss of her firstborn, flew on two

major aerial survey flights, traveled extensively in Europe, and saw the publication of two best-selling travel books.

Theme and Structure

The most intensive poetry-writing periods seem to have occurred during transitional phases of her life and at times when she was not involved in other major writing projects. From 1931 to 1938, when she was accompanying her husband to the Orient and to Europe and Africa, and when she was preparing books about those flights, she wrote few poems and published none. From 1939 to 1941, when she was involved in noninterventionist activities and working on her noninterventionist essays, eight poems were published. Then followed a four-year period (1942–1945), when she was writing *The Steep Ascent*, in which no poems appeared. From 1946 to 1957, however, over twenty poems were published.

In 1956 *The Unicorn and Other Poems* was published by Pantheon Books. This volume consists of thirty-five poems written from 1935 to 1955. The majority of them had previously appeared in the *Atlantic Monthly*; a smaller number had appeared in the *Saturday Review, Ladies Home Journal,* and *Vogue.*

The poem groupings in *The Unicorn and Other Poems* mark the important events and activities in which Lindbergh is most interested: love, death, restrictions to personal freedom, creative escape, cyclic patterns in life. The settings most frequently employed in the poems include the seaside, the open sky, and the winter landscape. The bare winter tree is an important symbol of spiritual strength, personal renewal, and economy of living, indicative of Lindbergh's Quaker outlook and preferred New England environment. The central poem of the book, "The Unicorn in Captivity," is a revealing personal statement of endurance under adverse conditions.

The thirty-five poems in the book are arranged in six sections: "Love," which consists of seven poems; "Death," eight poems; "Captive Spirit," seven poems; "The Unicorn," one longer poem; "Open Sky," six poems; and "Wind of Time," six poems. This arrangement is more thematic than chronological in order of composition, although most of the earlier poems are to be found in the first half of the book. The poems in the collection address issues and ideas that Lindbergh developed over the twenty years during which they were written, and while the specific events that may have occasioned them are personal and unique, the themes are universal. The logic of the titles and sequence of the six sections become clear as we examine the poems. Collectively and individually they describe a pattern of freedom, restriction, and accommodation; the central poem, "The Unicorn in Captivity," especially illustrates this pattern.

"Love," a motivating force, begins the process of personal development and establishment of relationships. "Death" follows love and confronts its life with the inevitable closure that time brings. "Captive Spirit" results from the constraints of closure upon love, as in her life it resulted from the effects of public attention upon her activities with her husband. "Unicorn" focuses upon the reactions of the spirit in captivity especially as they pertain to Lindbergh, the unicorn serving as a unique symbol of the poet herself. "Open Sky" explores the avenues of movement available to the captive spirit and is linked to the concept of restriction expressed in "Unicorn." "Wind of Time" sums up the poet's personal and creative progress.

Love

The first poem in the "Love" section, "The Man and the Child," establishes contrasts of age and youth, work and play, fear and love. The man (stanza one) works and fears, "doubts his neighbor," and "wears a mask"; he "moves in armor" and "hides his tears" (*UP,* 9). The child (stanza two), in contrast, plays and loves, is "open and maskless," "simple with trust." The movement of the poem, from the protective stance of adulthood to the accepting attitude of childhood, invites us to return to the emotional honesty and freshness of our youth, a necessary starting point for establishing a love relationship, and an intellectual advantage for one beginning to read a collection of poems.

"The Little Mermaid" is a balladlike parable of a woman's growth to adulthood and of the losses of the pleasures of youth. The seriousness of the message is balanced by the lightness of the meter and rhyme and by the children's story narrative. The poem is about the sacrifices that are made for love: "Only the little mermaid knows the price / One pays for mortal love . . ." (11). The sea-change associated with adult commitment brings the loss of youthful, magical attributes:

> The magic sweetness of a mermaid's song,
> She must abandon, if she would belong
> To mortal world . . . .

> . . . the mermaid's coral heart
> That felt no pain, she now must do without,
> Exchanged for mortal longing, mortal doubt.
>
> (12)

The concluding poem in this section, "Interior Tree," initially appeared in the November 1947 issue of *Atlantic Monthly* with the title of "Burning Tree." It repeats the image of the bare tree or, in this case, the tree in the process of becoming bare. The tree, according to the description in the poem, comes most vigorously alive as winter approaches, as its leaves display their bright autumnal coloring:

> Burning tree upon the hill
> And burning tree within my heart,
> What kinship stands between the two,
> What cord I cannot tear apart?
>
> The passionate gust that sets one free,
> —A flock of leaves in sudden flight—
> Shatters the bright interior tree
> Into a shower of splintered light.
>
> Fused moments of felicity,
> When flame in eye and heart unite,
> Come they from earth, or can they be
> The swallows of eternity?
>
> (18)

The image of the tree laden with leaves in bright fall colors depicts the last, glorious moment of life before the onset of winter, and the corresponding sensation in the poet suggests that the most profound moments of perception and understanding occur during the relatively brief transition from activity to inactivity, from growth to stagnancy. The "passionate gust that sets one free," the impulse of love, figuratively releases the leaves from the tree and perception from the soul in an explosion of light. The unexpected appearance of the swallows in the last line of the poem reinforces the notion of the quickness of the moment in addition to providing a magical visual transformation as leaves spring into life as swift-winged birds. The swallow as the harbinger of eternity offers hope for the life to come beyond the winter, death. The poem serves as a fitting transition to the next section, "Death."

Death

The poems in this section focus upon death, but although their
mood is generally somber, they also offer hope for renewal after death.
Like "Interior Tree," "All Saints' Day" celebrates the transition from
the end of summer to the onset of winter, of which the crucial event
is the "miracle" of death, a miracle every living thing experiences in
varying degrees of enlightenment. All Saints' Day, the first day of November, is the one day in which the events of that transition are most
clearly focused:

> Today no breath
>   Of life's allowed
> For Autumn spins
>   Her silken shroud.
>
> Thread upon thread
>   The earth is bound
> (November's needle
>   Makes the round).
>
> . . . .
>
> Earth waits a miracle—
>   Man too;
> This is the day
>   All saints pass through.
>   (30–31)

Because we all must eventually "pass through" the autumns of our
lives, we will all become "saints" and will experience our individual
miracles. The idea of the purification of the self as a link to sainthood
is evident in practically every one of Lindbergh's works after World
War II.

The last of the poems in this section, "Second Sowing," links the
general topic of death specifically to Lindbergh herself, for the poem
was written as a response to the death of her first son. Although it was
not published until 1948, it clearly relates the tragic events of 1932,
and in fact she placed the poem as a preface to her account of the year
1932 in the second volume of her published diaries and letters (HG,
219).

> Break down the bolted door;
> Rip open, spread and pour
> The grain upon the barren ground
> Wherever crack in clod is found.
>
> There is no harvest for the heart alone;
> The seed of love must be
> Eternally
> Resown.
>
> (32)

The harvest imagery links death to the autumn season, and the strength of the determination to sow a second crop channels the evident anger at the original act of violence into a creative and beneficial response. The poem concludes the "Death" section with the promise of life and provides an appropriate link to the following section, "Captive Spirit."

Captive Spirit

The central motif of "Captive Spirit" is of the limitation of personal fulfillment by duties and obligations, of peace by strife, of love by death. Closely associated with these conflicts is the sense of guilt that is often felt when one attempts to ignore limitations that are deemed socially acceptable. The first poem in the sequence, "Closing In," contrasts the supposed freedom of flying with the restrictive forces of weather and the terrain. One of three "Songs for Flying" originally published in the *Atlantic Monthly* in July 1947, "Closing In" blends lightness of tone and seriousness of theme:

> Just room for me to squeeze between
>   The lowered ceiling and divide,
> Just power enough to make the ridge
>   And, panting, gain the other side;
>
> Just light enough to see my field
>   And in the shadows kiss the grass;
> Just strength, just heart, just time enough,
>   For me, the tardy one, to pass.
>
> O hill, O strip of clearing sky,
>   Hold up the bars till I get by!
> O lovely day—forgive my sin,
>   One breath of light will let me in!
>
> (35)

The poem first describes a meteorological condition familiar to aviators, in which lowering clouds threaten to prevent the aircraft from flying over an approaching ridge. In the second stanza the fading light is reducing the visibility that will allow the pilot to land the aircraft safely. The deteriorating flying conditions are specifically linked to the moral condition of the pilot; her tardiness has apparently been caused by some unnamed failure of action or spirit, serious enough to be considered a "sin." The pilot's aeronautical predicament is the result not of incomplete flight preparation but of a failure of character. The omniscient world of nature thus is punishing the aviator. Salvation is still possible, however; a benevolent wind ("one breath of light") could improve conditions so that a safe landing could be made. If deliverance is possible, the meaning of the word *just* in the second stanza shifts from "barely" to "fair." The poet's concern about her lateness (she is "the tardy one") is reminiscent of similar fears expressed in *Listen! the Wind* and *The Steep Ascent*.

Lindbergh's noninterventionist voice is heard in the fourth poem in the section, "No Harvest Ripening," published initially in the autumn of 1939. This early poem compares the war in Europe to the season of the year; both are times of death and reawakening.

> Come quickly, winter, for the heart belies
> The truth of these warm days. These August skies
> Are all too fair to suit the times—so kind
> That almost they persuade the treacherous mind
> It still is summer and the world the same.
>
> (40)

The poem concludes with the observation that without the arrival of the winter following the autumn of the war, spiritual and cultural renewal will not be possible:

> Only with winter-patience can we bring
> The deep-desired, long-awaited spring.
>
> (41)

The relation of the ideas in "No Harvest Ripening" to *The Wave of the Future* is evident, for there Lindbergh argues that Western civilization requires the revitalization brought on by the revolution in political activity associated with her "wave of the future"; here, the winter season is necessary for renewal.

Unicorn

The section entitled "Unicorn" consists of one long poem, "The Unicorn in Captivity," and is subtitled "After the tapestry in The Cloisters." The poem is a verse description of the seventh panel of "The Hunt of the Unicorn" tapestry, hanging in the Cloisters of the Metropolitan Museum of Art in New York. A picture of the panel can be found on the cover of recent paperback reissues of the book. The scene is of the unicorn narrowly confined inside a red wooden fence in a field of hundreds of brightly colored flowers. The unicorn appears to be resting on its rear legs with front legs raised. The unicorn is facing to the observer's left, and its eyes appear to be fixed on something in the sky. A pomegranate tree, loaded with fruit, is located within the fenced-in area immediately behind the unicorn. The unicorn is secured to the pomegranate tree by a golden chain connected to a richly decorated leather strap fastened around its neck.

Consisting of nine stanzas varying in length from eleven to twenty-two lines, the poem celebrates the freedom the unicorn enjoys even in captivity. Lindbergh's synthesis of the visual elements in the scene described above is surprising, disturbing, and profound. Her account of the scene in the poem itself is especially thorough; no detail is overlooked. The opening twelve lines establish the visual and thematic context of the poem. The chase has ended, and the unicorn has been captured. Wounded by the king's spears, it has been secured to the pomegranate tree:

> Here sits the Unicorn
> In captivity;
> His bright invulnerability
> Captive at last . . . .
>
> (51)

Although it seems that the situation depicted should create a sense of despair, the poet injects a surprisingly optimistic note by suggesting at the conclusion of the first stanza that the unicorn has found a condition of freedom, not captivity:

> Here sits the Unicorn
> In captivity,
> Yet free.
>
> (51)

The detail of the second stanza establishes the basic motif of the poem,
that of the condition of the fragile captivity in which the unicorn is
held:

> Here sits the Unicorn;
> His overtakelessness
> Bound by a circle small
> As a maid's embrace . . . .

"Pinioned" by a fence of "scarlet rail," the unicorn is held in place by
a structure "fragile as a king's crown" or a butterfly net (51–52). The
imagery links the unicorn to the ideas traditionally associated with it:
religious purity, maidenly chasteness, royal qualities, and aesthetic
beauty. The notion that the unicorn's "overtakelessness"could be in fact
bound by a maid's embrace suggests that the unicorn has allowed himself to enter a condition of captivity, one that it could easily slip, at
least in the terms of its confinement as described in the poem. This
impression is confirmed in the next stanza, as we are told that he could
easily "leap the corral," "splinter the fencing," and "shatter his prison
wall," if he chose to do so. But because his world is not the world of
his captors, as the fourth stanza tells us, he does not feel held in
captivity:

> Dream wounds, dream ties,
> Do not bind him there
> In a kingdom where
> He is unaware
> Of his wounds, of his snare.
>   (53)

The unicorn accepts his bonds because

> he does not choose
> What choice would lose.
>   (54)

His spirit remains free and is symbolized by his "luminous horn,"
which rises far above the confining arena. The horn is Lindbergh's symbol of intellectual achievement, of the creative imagination free to
work in spite of physical constraints. The horn, in the seventh stanza,
is likened to a "free hymn of love," a comet, a galley's prow, a lily, a

bird in flight, a fountain (55). Each of these objects represents an alternative form of imaginative release.

After the struggle of the hunt, captivity also provides a needed refuge, in which the initial urge of the unicorn, to fight back against pursuit, is tempered into an acceptance of the necessary condition of captivity, as the unicorn's

> need to kill
> Has died like fire,
> And the need to love
> Has replaced desire . . . .
>
> (56)

The concluding stanza of the poem describes the unicorn as contemplative and accepting, its life force transferred from its physical activity to its imaginative activity:

> Quiet, save for his horn;
> Alive in his horn;
> Horizontally,
> In captivity;
> Perpendicularly,
> Free.
>
> (57)

The litanylike line that begins the poem and that returns at regular intervals, "Here sits the Unicorn," is transformed at the conclusion into a thematic statement of acceptance:

> Here lives the Unicorn,
> In captivity,
> Free.
>
> (57)

In the poem Lindbergh ignores the details of other scenes in the tapestry. She tells us little of the episodes that precede or follow. Information about the hunt that resulted in the capture of the unicorn could be deduced from observation of the wounds in its side. Yet this particular scene, and this scene alone, was of central importance to her. It seems apparent that the unicorn represents her own sense of self; spiritual, feminine, literary, and aesthetic qualities traditionally associated with the unicorn are all present in her writings of this and earlier periods, and the sense of persecution and the condition of captivity could clearly be associated with her life as a result of her marriage to her well-known aviator husband.

One sign of the sense of restriction Lindbergh must have felt can be discerned in a comparison of the 1955 unicorn, a symbol of captivity, to the 1927 unicorn, a symbol of escape. In her 1927 poem the unicorn suggests a feeling of release unfettered by the demands of daily life; in 1955 the unicorn, which continues to represent imaginative release, is confined in a fenced environment, bound to the pomegranate tree from which it fed in its youth.

Open Sky

The title of the following section, "Open Sky," follows logically from "The Unicorn," for the unicorn could find true "felicity" only in "night-free infinity / Of sky and stars" (57). The six poems in this section convey the idea of the sky as the inspiration for an awareness of the possibilities and limitations of creative activity. "Winter Tree," the core poem of the section, offers a unified combination of visual image and poetic theory; the opening stanza uses as its central motif the bare oak tree in winter:

> Again the oak, bare, stripped and barren, brings
> More confirmation to the heart than Spring's
> Returning green; more courage to refind
> The winter-bones of spirit unobscured
> By summer-flesh of leaves. . . .
>
> What power hidden in the winter tree
> Can set the captive spirit running free . . . ?
>   (62)

The poem summarizes the tenets of Lindbergh's poetic and philosophic outlook—the need for a disciplined, winter outlook to balance emotional, summer, excesses; the life-giving spirit that flows at its greatest depth in conditions of captivity; and the sense that a finished work, whether it be a poem, a person, or a tree, will be defined by the shape it achieves in conditions of adversity. The point of view of the poem, and of most of the poems in the book, is something like a Puritan view but less harsh, more accepting. Its landscape is the New England landscape of the late fall and early winter. Though founded in a perspective of austerity, it also recognizes, but does not fully approve of, excess.

"Flight of Birds" shifts the perspective from the participant (as in "Ascent") to the observer, as the verse form returns to Lindbergh's preferred mode for philosophical statement—iambic pentameter. The poet sees in a flight of birds both a common natural sight and a challenge to the powers of human interpretation:

> It is not fate in these external signs
> We read; it is ourselves—ourselves we see,
> Transmuted into bird or cloud or tree . . . .
> (70)

The conclusion of the poem suggests that the most profound insight that an event witnessed in nature can offer will occur when the event, its meaning, and the spectator are merged in a fused experience of life and death. That occasion will be a "miracle" in which "The heart reborn upon a flight of birds / Can now accept and recognize in words" (71).

"Back to the Islands" (72–73) concludes this section with a description of the poet's participation in the kind of experience envisioned in "Flight of Birds." Its island setting also serves to link *The Unicorn and Other Poems* with *Gift from the Sea*, published the previous year.

Wind of Time

The collection concludes with the section entitled "Wind of Time," in which the wind, like a living river, links past, present, and future, in a continuum where experiences are continually changing yet remaining the same. "Presentiment," which begins the section, offers the familiar image of the autumn tree (77). The poem links the poet's thoughts to the movement of a leaf on the tree and correlates remembrances of the past and concerns for the future.

"Within the Wave" presents the condensed vision of the present as an instant between the past and the future, the framed image of the world within the wave reinforced in the poem's sonnet form:

> Smooth mirror of the present, poised between
> The crest's "becoming" and the foam's "has been"—
> How luminous the landscape seen across
> The crystal lens of an impending loss!
> (78)

The symbolic function of the wave in the poem is much the same as it was in Lindbergh's earlier essay, *The Wave of the Future.* The theme of the merging of the past, present, and future is continued in "Family Album" as the poet examines an old photograph of her newly married parents from the viewpoint of child and parent simultaneously. The poet's description of her mother as a young bride illustrates the theme of the blending of the past and present and embodies it at the same time as the perspectives of the child and grandmother merge:

> I am no longer daughter gazing back;
> I am your mother, watching far ahead,
> Seeing events so clearly now they're gone . . . .
>
> . . . . . .
>
> Mother compassionate and child bereft
> I am; the past and present, wisdom and innocence,
> Fused by one flicker of a camera lens . . . .
>   (80–81)

The final section of the book concludes with "Bare Tree," in which the image of the autumn tree, stripped of leaves and anticipating the onset of winter, once again reappears. That this image is the central symbol of Lindbergh's poetic work is evident from its repeated occurrence in the poems in the book. In this final instance, however, the image is directly associated with the poet, as she visualizes herself providing insight for others as she prepares for her own eventual death:

> Already I have shed the leaves of youth,
> Stripped by the wind of time down to the truth
> Of winter branches. Linear and alone
> I stand, a lens for lives beyond my own,
> A frame through which another's fire may glow,
> A harp on which another's passion, blow.
>
> . . . . . .
>
> Blow through me, Life, pared down at last to bone,
> So fragile and so fearless have I grown!
>   (86)

The Ciardi review

The publication of *The Unicorn and Other Poems* occasioned a scathing review by John Ciardi, newly assigned poetry editor of the *Saturday Review of Literature*. Ciardi, a poet of some distinction, had been added to the editorial staff of the *Saturday Review* by Norman Cousins, who had himself recently been appointed editor of the magazine. Ciardi apparently felt that a new set of critical standards for evaluating poetry was appropriate for postwar readers; his critical viewpoint became evident in the 12 January 1957 issue of the *Saturday Review*, in which he announced that Lindbergh's *The Unicorn and Other Poems* was "miserable stuff" (57). Ciardi's review, which covered the better part of three pages, contained no favorable comments regarding the poems in the volume, and neglected to mention the major poem in the collection, "The Unicorn in Captivity."

The public response to the review was one of outrage. The editorial offices of the *Saturday Review* were flooded with letters, the majority of which were severely critical of Ciardi. Editor Norman Cousins felt that the outcry required acknowledgment, and his two-page response appeared three weeks later, in the 2 February issue. In his response Cousins defended Ciardi's right to deliver his editorial opinions, but he made clear his disagreement with Ciardi's assessment of Lindbergh's poetry. Cousins objected to the manner, tone, and critical basis of Ciardi's review. But the controversy did not end with Cousins's response, for in the same issue appeared Ciardi's reply to those readers who had complained of Ciardi's harsh evaluation. Even in the title of his rebuttal it was clear that Ciardi was not about to apologize; his response was entitled "The Reviewer's Duty to Damn; A Letter to an Avalanche." Ciardi quoted a number of excerpts from some of the letters, the tenor of which was that Ciardi was a bad critic and a bad person. But this overwhelmingly pro-Lindbergh response appeared only to feed Ciardi's ire, not to mitigate it, and he reiterated his opinion of the poems in *The Unicorn* in even stronger language than that of the original review. But even as he was completing his second attack on the Lindbergh poems, evidence of a larger target than *The Unicorn* appeared:

More urgently, however, I am trying to establish as a policy of this magazine that poetry is a serious, dignified, and disciplined human activity, which is not to be debased in the name of a counterfeit sentimentality that will not bother to learn the fundamentals of its own art. (25)

Ciardi's attack was unfortunate primarily because his review drew more attention to itself than to the poems it was intended to evaluate, and the atmosphere of acrimonious partisanship it created made it almost impossible to read the poems with detachment. It is doubtful that we will ever know the real reason for the virulence of Ciardi's attack on *The Unicorn;* it does not seem likely that his determination to alter the magazine's editorial policy would have in itself necessitated the harsh language he employed in the original review and in the rebuttal that followed. Certainly Lindbergh must have been hurt by the attack, for it illustrated exactly the effects of the kind of limiting forces she had referred to in "The Unicorn in Captivity" and other poems in the volume.

Lindbergh published only one more poem after the controversy created by the Ciardi review subsided. Entitled "Mid-summer," it was published in the December 1957 issue of the *Atlantic Monthly,* nine months after the Ciardi review appeared. Perhaps the Ciardi attack and the subsequent controversy are responsible for the poem's relatively somber, even bitter tone.

The Unicorn and Other Poems constitutes a complete and unified poetic achievement. *The Unicorn* is Lindbergh's poetic testament; it encompasses and describes her life and poetic vision. The structure of the book is clearly planned, and the themes of freedom, restriction, and continuity are carefully interwoven. The book gains momentum poem by poem, section by section, offering a complete version of the poet's philosophic beliefs and poetic achievement.

Chapter Eleven
Dearly Beloved

Dearly Beloved combines philosophical discourse in a fictional framework. In its thematic outlook it is a logical development of the meditations on self and personal relationships begun in *Gift from the Sea,* and in its construction it is a variation on the approach employed in *The Steep Ascent.* It has much in common with the works of Virginia Woolf, one of Lindbergh's favorite authors, for, as in Woolf's work, it combines a conventional event with an unconventional narrative device. In this case the narrative device is a series of meditations, provided by nine participants at the wedding of Sally McNeil and Mark Gallatin. The individual narratives are devoted to the subject of marriage, and provide differing perspectives on personal happiness in marriage. Taken in sum, they present a spectrum of marital attitudes and beliefs. Because the nine narrators represent a full range of ages and backgrounds, the book offers a comprehensive catalogue of views of the institution of marriage.

In 1962 the Lindbergh children ranged in age from thirty (the age of Jon, the eldest) to seventeen (the age of Reeve, the youngest). The two oldest children, Jon and Land, were married, and 1962 was the year in which Anne, the third child and oldest daughter, was married. The two youngest, Scott and Reeve, were fast approaching marriage age. So it is not surprising that Anne Lindbergh's *Dearly Beloved,* published in 1962, should have marriage as its subject.

Dearly Beloved is in many ways a departure from her earlier works, but in many ways it is very much like them. Subtitled *A Theme and Variations,* it examines the marriage relationship from a number of differing perspectives presented in the thoughts and comments of the members of a wedding party. Unlike *The Steep Ascent,* which Lindbergh acknowledged as a thinly disguised version of a factual occurrence in her life, *Dearly Beloved* describes a marriage ceremony that could occur in any upper middle-class household in America.

The novel's three-part structure results from the relatively brief chronological sequence of events encompassing the wedding ceremony of Sally McNeil and Mark Gallatin, held on a June afternoon in the house of the bride's parents. The first portion of the novel, the first three chapters, describes events immediately preceding the wedding ceremony. The second, and longest, section consists of nine chapters of individual voices heard during the ceremony. The closing section, the final four chapters, describes the concluding events of the wedding, the wedding supper, and the departure of the wedding guests.

The central section of the novel is the most complex, as each of the nine chapters is told from the viewpoint of a different member of the wedding party. Each guest reflects on his or her own marital or extra-marital relationships or on the relationships of others represented at the ceremony. Each of the nine narratives is stylistically distinctive, and the views of love, marriage, and marital relations represented in them range from naive to cynical, from idealistic to disillusioned. Each viewpoint is different and each mode of expression is highly individualized. Both contrasting and complementary viewpoints are presented so that, taken in sum, the nine chapters offer nine "variations" on the theme of marriage. Although the novel is not lengthy, Lindbergh creates subtle and complex patterns of interpersonal relationships that illuminate and explore traditional notions of love.

The individual around whom the action flows is the bride's mother, Deborah McNeil. The opening and closing sections of the novel are narrated chiefly by her, and hers is the first narrative voice to be heard in the extended middle section. In the opening chapter, "Before," Deborah reflects on the short-term and long-term effects that the wedding of her daughter, the eldest of her four children, will have upon the family. This section establishes the personalities of the central members of the McNeil family. In the next two chapters of the opening section, "In This Company" and "The Wedding March," thoughts and comments of other members of the wedding party are blended into the narrative, as their opinions and ideas force themselves into the flow of the group's consciousness. When the processional begins, a slowed time sequence allows the members of the wedding party to become involved in extended reveries that are prompted by phrases from the wedding service, the first words of which, "Dearly Beloved, we are gathered together," signal the beginning of the middle portion of the novel.

The Family Groupings

In one important aspect the book is less like a novel and more like a series of individualized essays in which each family member or friend presents one aspect of the issue. Adding to the intricacy of the narrative technique is the fact that numerous members of seven different family groupings are introduced at one point or another. Because there is no crisis in the plot development—indeed there is very little plot at all, in the traditional sense—identification of individual family members is important for an understanding of the themes and ideas in the book.

Altogether nearly fifty individual characters are identified by name, over twenty of whom display reasonably well-developed personalities. The family members from both houses—the McNeils and the Gallatins—represent a variety of marital conditions: some are happily married, some are unhappily married, some are single, and some are divorced. In addition, friends of the Gallatin family add a Continental perspective to the attitudes toward marriage that appear in the narrative.

The Nine Individual Narratives

Five of the nine speakers of the individual narratives are women; four are men. The attitudes conveyed by these nine individuals range from hope and envy to cynicism and despair. The viewpoints expressed balance one another nicely, each typically functioning as a kind of counterpoint to the one previously given, each a different variation on the theme of marital compatibility. Although a number of pessimistic views on the survivability of marriage are expressed, the final impression is one of belief in marriage as an essential bond between two caring individuals.

The first narrative voice is that of Deborah McNeil. Deborah reflects on Sally's youthful days and her own married life with John McNeil. Although she is generally satisfied with their life together, she wishes for a more significant life than the one she has been living lately. For Deborah, "communication with another person" is the "realest thing in life" (*DB*, 34). Deborah considers that her marriage to John is solid, if not exciting, and she is willing to settle for that quality.

The next narrative voice is that of Don, married to Deborah's sister Henrietta. A psychologist, Don knows too much of marital troubles through his work and in himself to be able to see marriage as a perfect state. His is the most cynical, and most modern, voice in the book. His views of marriage as an institution contrast markedly with the idealistic meditations of Deborah and serve as an immediate antidote to the views Deborah has expressed. He is the first to consider the importance of sexual relations in marriage. Don's emphasis on the unavoidable necessity of the physical relationship serves as a healthy corrective to the occasionally excessive idealism of Deborah's narrative.

Aunt Harriet, Deborah's elderly aunt, provides the narrative voice of the next chapter. Aunt Harriet, who has never married, represents the Gardiner New England heritage, as she recalls the experiences of her sister and brother and of her parents in years long past. Aunt Harriet serves as a link to the past, both to prior generations and the standards they represented, but more especially as a reminder of the inexorable march of time, of the eventual approach of death. If there were any one individual Lindbergh might have had in mind as a model for Aunt Harriet, it might well have been Mary Ellen Chase, her literature teacher at Smith College and writer of several books about New England life, chief among which was *A Goodly Heritage.*

The fourth narrative voice is that of Chrissie, Sally McNeil's bridesmaid, as the perspective shifts from age to youth, from reflections on the past to hopes for the future. Chrissie's narrative provides the necessary background for an understanding of how Sally and Mark met, and the language of the narrative is that of youth, of current 1962 expressions and courtship rituals. Chrissie's interest in the sexual aspect of marriage is linked to Don's reflections on the subject two chapters earlier; Chrissie's eager anticipation balances Don's cynical assessment, and both narratives balance the idealistic reflections of Deborah and Aunt Harriet.

The next narrative voice is that of André, the young French visitor to America, and although his perspective is also that of youth, his European upbringing has given him a more sophisticated insight into the complexities of marriage than appears in Chrissie's vision. André's thoughts are primarily concentrated on the contrast between the French and American modes of life; the French approach is more structured, more traditional. André's concern over the different kinds of life represented by France and America serves as a contrast to the exclusively American perspective of Chrissie's narrative by revealing another kind of modern outlook, one derived from a cultural emphasis on continuity and responsibility.

Beatrice Locke's narrative follows next, as the events of the marriage are seen by someone who has experienced the trauma of divorce and the joy of a happy second marriage. Beatrice's narrative contains one of the most satisfactory descriptions of a happy relationship to be found in the book; her description of her realization of her true self, which came to her as a result of her divorce, is especially effective. It is evident that in the novel Beatrice's divorce is equated to a personal inability to fulfill the American dream of ideal marriage. Yet it is also evident that of all the couples attending the wedding ceremony, Beatrice and her second husband, Spencer Locke, are the happiest. Beatrice has undergone the full range of marital pressures and has shown that not only is it possible to survive the breakup of a marriage, the dissolution of one marriage can lead to a happier life in another.

The seventh narrative voice is that of Pierre, André's uncle. Like André, Pierre sees the wedding ceremony from a continental perspective, but from a more experienced point of view. Pierre, with his European education, is the logical choice to express the ideas of two of Lindbergh's favorite continental writers, Rilke and Saint-Exupéry; Pierre recalls the Rilke notion of "two solitudes, who protect and touch and greet each other" (129), but he prefers Saint-Exupéry's idea that "love does not consist in gazing at each other, but in looking outward together in the same direction" (130). The reappearance of the ideas of the two writers who were most often quoted in *Gift from the Sea* establishes the philosophical and thematic links between the two books.

Frances Gallatin, the eighth narrator, is unhappily married to a talented artist who drinks too much, but she has decided to remain in her marriage and not to seek a divorce, as Beatrice did. Frances represents the viewpoint of a woman who believes in the importance of the institution as a basis for stability and meaning in family life. She offers a complementary perspective to that of Beatrice, who has opted for divorce as a solution to an unhappy situation.

The last of the nine individualized perspectives, that of Deborah's father, Theodore Gardiner, is the most all-encompassing, the most spiritual. The philosophers whose ideas he recalls during his narrative include St. Augustine, Christ, and Plato. But more important than the expressions of the classical philosophers is Theodore's own philosophical view, in which he sees love as "a stream of compassion which fed the world" (159). As he looks at the gathered friends and relatives, Theodore discovers only one couple whose sense of marital compatibility matches the one he has shared with his dying wife–Beatrice and

Spencer Locke. Theodore represents the closing of the loop, the completion of the cycle in the story, for he simultaneously looks back to
the past and forward to the future. He also encompasses all the other
narrative figures in his vision and philosophical outlook; recognizing
their weaknesses and their strengths, he accepts them for what they are
and does not judge them against unrealistic standards. His concluding
thought serves as a kind of thematic benediction to the wedding
ceremony:

Weddings, he said to himself, expressed the eternal hope of the human
race. . . . For a wedding was not only a promise and a pledge made in the
eye of God and man; it was a heightening of human life by the addition of
something beyond it, something uncertain, intangible, impossible to prove.
An assertion of man's belief in a quality of spirit—love. (174)

The first of the final chapters, "Bride and Groom," describes an episode
of music and dancing with which the wedding ceremony ends. The
second, "The Supper," is narrated from Deborah's perspective, as she
takes pleasure in realizing that she has had a large part in helping to
make the day a success, and that she has been able to invest the ceremony with companionship and significance. The next chapter, "The
Toast," is related primarily from Frances's point of view, as the mother
of the bridegroom reaffirms her sense of the value of the marriage relationship that she felt during the wedding service. In the final chapter, "After," the bride and groom depart, and the McNeil household
begins to return to a new mode of normalcy.

Symbol and Metaphor

The book celebrates an important event; the wedding ceremony is a
meaningful experience, in spite of the uncertainty of individual marital
relationships. In addition to the "variations" on the theme of marriage
that the story offers, Lindbergh also builds into the novel a number of
interrelated symbols and metaphors that reinforce the idea of the value
of marriage as a personal and familial ceremony. The most important
of these is the symbol of the web and the metaphor of the stream.

The web is mentioned often in the story, serving as a visual symbol
of the interrelationships among the people who are present at the wedding. In addition, the web suggests the inextricable ways in which
daily activities are linked to and build from the practical and philo-

sophical basis of marriage. The image of the web is introduced early, in the third chapter, "The Wedding March," as the opening lines of the service, "Dearly beloved, we are gathered together," begin the important central section of the book; "This was the gathering point. All the strands were drawn together at this moment, pulled taut, tied in a knot of supreme tension" (20).

When Beatrice thinks of the relationship of Deborah and John, she considers that "consciously or unconsciously, they had made a web of relationship that held and fed their children" (109). And when she recalls her divorce, she thinks of its effects on her daughter: "To destroy the web [of marriage] was a sin" (112). Finally, she views the "endless small interplay of daily tasks" as "the substance of life itself, the web of marriage, as important as the bigger things, even an expression of them" (119).

The description of love as a stream of life is a continuous theme that runs through the book. It is introduced first in a scene in which Deborah remembers her father discussing the subject: "Love," Theodore says, "is the stream of compassion which feeds the world. . . . When you are in the stream and part of it," he said, "it feeds you, and everything you do and give is the stream flowing through you. You are a channel for love; you love, and people love you; it is all effortless" (39). Even the cynical Don thinks of love as something that flows (50), and the concept is one to which both Deborah and Theodore refer later in the wedding ceremony.

Another important issue that recurs frequently is the notion of the true experience in a love relationship, often described as the "real thing," the essential quality of a shared relationship. The "real thing" is variously defined by different individuals; most often it is thought of as some kind of magic moment of true communication between the two partners. By the end of the marriage ceremony, however, it has become transformed into a complex concept that blends elements of communication and communion. Deborah first thinks of the "real thing" as something that "never got said" (10). Later she associates it with communication between her and her husband: "Communication with another person—wasn't it the realest thing in life?" (34). When Chrissie wonders about the "real thing" (82), she associates it with some secret that has not been told her about sex or love (85), something she will have to discover for herself. Beatrice sees the "real thing" as the self stripped bare of surface personalities: "All loves led to the final love, to the final stripping away of the unreal selves, to the true meet-

ing" (115). To Frances, however, the "real thing" was her husband
Stephen when she first met him, before his process of dissipation began
(142).

For Deborah, these concepts and symbols are interrelated in the
wedding supper, when she is able to gather friends and relatives, young
and old, together at one table to share, however imperfectly, food and
conversation:

> The phrase "the community of marriage" came to her from the old-fashioned
> past. *Community* was what they had together. And perhaps this was the mean-
> ing of marriage, not the communication she was forever looking for. Com-
> munity—communion—communication: the words might be closer than she
> knew. (186).

Throughout the novel there is an awareness of the cyclic nature of
things, of youth becoming middle-aged, of middle age becoming old;
all processes and relationships share these cyclic qualities, of sequences
beginning and ending in a natural and unsurprising order. The cyclic
nature of events is reflected in the motif of music, which so thoroughly
infiltrates the wedding ceremony from beginning to end; the service
begins with the traditional wedding march and ends with a dance, in
which all present are invited to move with a partner to the measure of
time, in imitation of the processes of life itself. The awareness of the
inevitable triumph of death is maintained in a consistent yet unobtru-
sive fashion throughout the story.

  Dearly Beloved shares a number of similarities with Lindbergh's earlier work of fiction, *The Steep Ascent*. As in the earlier work, the primary
narrator is a woman whose primary concern is the establishment of a
meaningful family relationship. Although Eve Alcott in *The Steep Ascent* is pregnant, and Deborah McNeil is about to see her eldest daughter married, the concerns of the two women narrators are essentially
the same: providing a base of support from which the family relationship can continue to grow. *Dearly Beloved* is more successful in the way
it incorporates its cast of characters and the many personal issues with
which they are engrossed than is *The Steep Ascent*.

  Even though we are being offered a work of fiction, Lindbergh's
method is much like the approach of *Gift from the Sea,* for the narrators
make cogent observations and present convincing conclusions based

upon their personal experiences in their own marriage relationships. The logic leading to these conclusions is made readily available to us as readers; our challenge is to debate those conclusions by entering into a mental discourse with them, as we try to discover for ourselves exactly what we think the "real thing" is that lies at the heart of an enduring marriage relationship.

Chapter Twelve
Earth Shine

With the publication of *Earth Shine* Lindbergh brings her works full cycle, for the two essays that constitute the book, a 1966 examination of African wildlife and a 1969 description of an Apollo moon launch, offer an instructive variation on the aerial travel narratives with which she began her writing career. Like the early works, these essays describe the Lindberghs' travels to previously unexplored areas, the African game preserves and the Cape Kennedy launch site. But they have exchanged the novelty of rapid air travel for the slower-paced life of travel on foot or by automobile. The emphasis in the *Earth Shine* essays is not on new locales and unusual peoples, but on the natural environment, on the birds and animals, and on the potentially disturbing effects of human activity on wildlife habitats. In her earlier works Lindbergh had been vitally concerned with the importance of perception, as she wrote about her determined efforts to understand fully the sights she witnessed on their travels. And although the thematic message has changed little—she is still concerned with her ability to see the world as clearly as possible—now the emphasis is not on symbol or submerged meanings, but on the direct visual evidence nature offers.

Lindbergh's interest in conservation issues resulted from her observation of the natural environment over which she flew, but she wrote about the subject later in her life, after she and her husband became active in environmental issues. From the early 1960s until his death in 1975 Charles Lindbergh devoted greater amounts of his time to anthropological explorations, especially into Africa and the Philippines. He became increasingly committed to the conservation of natural resources, a commitment shared by his wife.

As early as the summer of 1941 Lindbergh warned her readers, in "Reaffirmation," of the possible detrimental effects of technological developments. An important part of that essay, which was primarily intended as a reply to critics of *The Wave of the Future,* was her effort to draw attention to the fact that the public seemed to have accepted without question the ever-increasing effects of technology in the world.

In connection with the revolutionary forces she sensed were evolving in the world, she urged that her readers consider the merits of regaining control of the machine:

The revolution that will have to take place over the world before it can again begin its march forward seems to me not alone the conquest of machine by man, but much more deeply the conquest of spirit over matter. The material world has outstripped us, and we must try to make up our lost ground. (*Atlantic Monthly* 167 [June 1941], 686)

In an age in which belief in technology and the value of the machine was still strong, Lindbergh had the vision to warn against the unquestioning acceptance of technological innovation. This cautionary view of technological improvements was allied to a growing belief in the value of preserving the natural life of the planet.

Lindbergh's ecological writings consist primarily of three essays she wrote from 1966 through 1970, the two essays for *Life* that constitute *Earth Shine* and a 1970 address she gave to the graduating class of Smith College, published later under the title of "Harmony with the Life Around Us." The address has as its central theme the idea that the "artificial split between man and nature has been responsible not only for many of the physical, social and economic troubles of our time, but it has also resulted in great moral and spiritual distress" (*Good Housekeeping* 171 [July 1970], 62). Lindbergh urges her audience to become actively involved in the effort to recognize and protect the nation's resources. She suggests that the reaction against the war in Vietnam has resulted from "a deep instinctive protest against the growing dehumanization of our world—against an industrialized, mechanized civilization in which the flame of life itself is sputtering" (150). This sentiment is consistent with her postwar comments about the impact of World War II on European life.

But Lindbergh suggests that science and technology by themselves should not be blamed for the misuse of world resources. "Technology is not going to cure itself," she points out, adding that "the so-called cures are often more disastrous than the complaints!" (152). Science, she says, "can only inform us about our world. It can bring us knowledge but it cannot set up values. Values are created by individuals" (152). Lindbergh's strong ecological and resource-oriented stand evolved naturally, over a number of years, as she observed and wrote of the potential damage that uncontrolled technology could create in the world. Her interest in the subject had been demonstrated as early as her postwar essays of 1947 and 1948, but it is most strongly in evidence in two essays she wrote for *Life* in 1966 and 1969.

"Immersion in Life"

Lindbergh's 1966 essay, titled "Immersion in Life; a Brief Safari Back to Innocence," was published in the 21 October 1966 issue of *Life*. In that year members of the Lindbergh family visited the animal preserves in Kenya and Tanzania, in East Africa, where for a month they observed the habits of a variety of wildlife living there—lions, zebras, giraffes, elands, elephants, gazelles. The essay at first seems to be a kind of travel narrative, an account of the highlights of the Lindberghs' African trip, with its vivid descriptions of Nairobi National Park, the Highlands of Kenya, the extinct volcanic crater of Ngorongoro, and the Olduvai Gorge. But its deeper purpose is to provide a sense of inundation in the variety and numbers of African wildlife, in direct contrast to the more familiar environment of urban America.

The Lindberghs were in the heart of what had once been big-game hunting country, in the vicinity of Mount Kilimanjaro; like Hemingway and others who had seen the area, Lindbergh was moved to write about her experiences. The essay examines the nature of the relationship between animals and people; as she says in the opening paragraphs, "I felt a connection with these animals I saw daily" (*Life* 61 [21 October 1966], 90). The interrelationship between humans and animals is developed in a series of contrasts that she witnesses in the East African environment: "Africa embraces both the bright and the dark, the benign and the cruel, the fleeting and the timeless, the swift and the ponderous . . . (94). Even the concept of time offers contrasts; Lindbergh thinks of "time as history and time as rhythm" (94). The pattern of contrasts established in the essay illustrates the conflicts of opposites that exist in daily African life: the hot noon and the cold nights; the peacefulness of the pastoral environment and the violence that occurs when the stronger form of wildlife feed on the weaker; the old world coexisting with the new; life and death: "Life and death, seen through the burning lens of Africa, are inextricably knotted. In the midst of such abundant life, death is absorbed and accepted; but never forgotten and hidden, as in more civilized worlds" (96). In the essay strongly contrasting elements are seen as providing an essential balance in the natural order of the world. The primitive honesty of life on the Serengeti plain illustrates these contrasts in their most obvious form.

The primary thematic message the essay conveys is one of *connections*, of the relationships between human life and animal life and of the interdependence of the two. The pattern of contrasts illustrates the natural excesses that can be forgotten in the comfortable environment of modern America. This point is made clear late in the essay, after the reader has been almost overwhelmed with scenes of natural life: "Animals are necessary to man, although man, insulated by his civilization, is often dulled to the need. . . . Immersion in wilderness life, like immersion in the sea, may return civilized man to a basic element from which he sprang and with which he has now lost contact" (97–98).

Lindbergh concludes by observing that in the imaginative act of visualizing the life and actions of the animal, one is participating in an essentially religious experience because "the act of obeisance to life" is essentially religious (98). Awareness of the often violently opposed extremes of which truly natural life consists, Lindbergh says, is important to our heightened sense of the value of life. The spiritual emphasis is continued in the essay that followed three years later.

"The Heron and the Astronaut"

The second of this paired set of essays, "The Heron and the Astronaut," appeared in the 28 February 1969 issue of *Life*. Its subject does not at first glance seem to correspond to the earlier essay, for the subject of the second essay is the Apollo 8 moon-orbiting mission, launched from Cape Kennedy, Florida, on 21 December 1968. But the pairing of the essay with the earlier article is appropriate, for it continues and expands Lindbergh's ideas of contrasts and continuities.

The Lindberghs had been invited to attend the Apollo launch by President Johnson, and Lindbergh delivered her essay to *Life* in a little over six weeks after the launch, a briefer production time than she was used to. The rapid response time was essential for reader interest, for in 1968 and 1969 moon shots were being launched in quick succession as the National Air and Space Administration (NASA) attempted to fulfill John F. Kennedy's 1960 promise to land a man on the moon "within a decade." Apollo 11, which carried Neil Armstrong to the surface of the moon, was carried out in July of 1969.

The title of the *Life* article, "The Heron and the Astronaut," indicates the central contrast of the essay, as the natural world of the heron

is juxtaposed to the technological world of the astronaut. Both crea-
tures fly, but one does so naturally, while the other is propelled by
technology. Throughout the essay images of natural and artificial life
are placed in opposition. Other contrasts, also found in "Immersion in
Life," are evident as well: the primitive and the modern, the old and
the new. The *Life* essay is partitioned into five segments: "The Setting," "The Night Before," "The Morning of Launching," "Afternoon—Merritt Island," and "Dialogue."

"The Setting," a long introductory section, begins with a reminis-
cence of a visit the Lindberghs had made to the launch area over
twenty-five years earlier, when it was called by its original name, Cape
Canaveral, an isolated expanse of sand and pine. The area now has been
heavily built up with highways, motels, gas stations, and restaurants.
The Lindberghs and other selected visitors are given a special tour of
the impressive launch facility, the Vehicle Assembly Building (VAB)
and the Launch Control Center (LCC). Later they are given the rare
opportunity to share lunch with the mission astronauts—Frank Bor-
man, James Lovell, Edward Anders—and other astronauts scheduled
for future space flights. Lindbergh describes her husband's reminis-
cences of his friendship with Robert Goddard, one of the pioneers in
American rocketry, who had predicted that a rocket could reach the
moon, but who also had predicted that the costs of doing so might be
prohibitively high—as much as one million dollars, a fraction of the
actual cost. The astronauts are understandably amused at this anecdote.
Charles Lindbergh is awed by the amount of fuel the launch vehicle
will consume; in the first second of flight, he figures, it will consume
ten times the amount *The Spirit of St. Louis* consumed when it flew
from New York to Paris in 1927.

The next section, "The Night Before," describes the Lindberghs'
nighttime visit to the launch pad, where the Apollo launch vehicle is
brightly lit by spotlights. Lindbergh visualizes the scene in anthropological terms; the mobile launcher, the device that holds the launch
vehicle, "almost seems to lean, with its overhanging crane, above the
slightly smaller rocket, in a gesture that is half embrace, half release;
while the rocket at its side is new-born, naked, silver-bright" (*Life* 66
[28 February 1969], 20). The rocket is described as a "seed, split from
its pod," about to begin its journey into space (20).

As she gazes at the impressive launch structure, Lindbergh is reminded of the passage in *The Education of Henry Adams,* when Adams
stood before the dynamo at the turn of the century, wondering whether

the physical power of the dynamo would replace the spiritual power of the Virgin. In her inclusion of Henry Adams's philosophical questions and her husband's recollections of his 1927 flight, Lindbergh establishes a historical and philosophical context against which to place the achievement of the Apollo launch.

The launch is described in the section entitled "The Morning of Launching." In the strong light of the morning Lindbergh now sees the launch vehicle as "no longer tender or biological, but simply a machine, the newest and most perfected creation of a scientific age—hard, weighty metal" (22). The first seconds of the launch are "like a dream" because the sound of the launch has not yet reached the viewing area; but when the noise of the launch is heard, it is almost unbearable in its earth-shaking intensity. As the sound slowly diminishes, Lindbergh notices flocks of startled birds circling out of nearby marshes.

After the launch the Lindberghs, feeling the need to "touch earth again," to "drench" themselves in nature, visit the Merritt Island Game Refuge, located within the Cape Kennedy area (22). In this section of the essay ("Afternoon—Merritt Island") Lindbergh describes the many varieties of bird and animal life they observe there. She is fascinated by the effect of the sudden shift in their surroundings. In the morning they were in the midst of a world of technology, and in the afternoon they are in the natural world: "We have passed into another frame of reference. The veil of civilization has become almost invisible. Instead of the mammoth gray-and-white VAB on the horizon, our eyes pick up white herons . . ." (23).

The progress of the moon flight is outlined in the section entitled "Dialogue," as Lindbergh essentially lets the astronauts speak for themselves, as they describe the scene they observe from their spacecraft windows.

In the concluding, untitled section of the essay Lindbergh attempts to place the achievement of the Apollo 8 flight, and of spaceflight in general, in her special historical and philosophical context. She shifts the focus away from an overemphasis upon the achievements of technology, reminding her readers that technological achievement has created new possibilities for philosophical insight and spiritual appreciation of the place of the human community in the universe. She prefers to see the successful Apollo flight as a sign that there is a possibility that the forces of technology can work in accord with the forces of nature to create a "renewed sense of harmony" in the world (26). Lindbergh's intent is essentially ameliorative; she chooses not to place technological and natural forces in opposition, but to see them instead as complementary halves of a unified whole in which both forces can function together successfully.

Consolidation and Revision

Later in 1969 the two essays were published together under the title *Earth Shine;* included in the book were many striking photographs, some in color, showing scenes of Cape Kennedy and Africa. The essays appear in the book in reverse chronological order; that is, "The Heron and the Astronaut" (1969) precedes "Immersion in Life" (1966). The effect of the reversal is to assist the thematic sequence of ideas in the two essays, for the comments in the concluding portion of "The Heron and the Astronaut" lead logically to a discussion of natural life on the planet, while the concluding comments of "Immersion in Life" serve well as a summary of the central ideas of both essays.

"Immersion in Life" was reprinted almost without any changes in the original text; the only noticeable difference in the book version is the omission of a topical reference to a major power failure that affected the east coast of the United States in 1966. "The Heron and the Astronaut," however, was significantly revised and rewritten. The most heavily revised portion of the original essay is the concluding section. The revisions in the final section are largely the result of a reordering of the material as well as a clarifying of the style. In the revised version the previously untitled concluding section is given a separate heading, entitled "Back to Earth." In addition to adding a concluding heading, Lindbergh also revised the original five headings slightly.

In the revised version approximately ten to fifteen paragraphs were added to the text to provide supplementary factual and historical information and to develop thematic meaning. Other additions give a clearer, more comprehensive picture of the launch facility itself; this material provides specific details of the December 1968 launch and of the launch facility.

Additional historical material is given primarily to illuminate the life and accomplishments of Robert Goddard, the American rocketry pioneer. Information about Goddard is expanded from one short paragraph in the original version to eight paragraphs in the final version (11–13). Goddard's name is introduced early in the revised version, where it serves to link recent technological developments with the research efforts conducted almost fifty years earlier. The additional material regarding Robert Goddard establishes a historical and technological basis for thematic development while it gives wider recognition to Goddard's achievements, recognition that the Lindberghs felt had been inadequate. Goddard becomes a historical presence whose work the Apollo launch serves to celebrate.

The second major section containing additional material is titled the "Dialogue—Earth and Moon," to which Lindbergh added more than six paragraphs of astronaut-controller conversation. This supplementary dialogue creates a clearer sense of the truly awesome aspect of the moon flight, as the astronauts' comments directly convey the excitement of the unique views of the earth and moon that they are able to witness.

The concluding section of the revised essay also contains many more reminders of the fact that the launch occurred during Christmas week of 1968. These additional comments serve to enhance the themes of harmony and goodwill that the essays develop. This increased emphasis reinforces other spiritual aspects that are present throughout the essay, especially in the concluding section.

In her preface specially written for *Earth Shine* Lindbergh suggests that these two essays, which at first glance appear to link unlike subjects, in fact describe complementary halves of a unified world view. She suggests that one looks outward to the moon to gain a clearer perspective of the earth in space, a perspective gained only with the assistance of technology; so also should one look inward, toward the earth, to gain a clearer understanding of the relationship of the human community and the natural environment. She relates an incident that occurred one night while they were seated around the campfire in Africa; they looked up into the nighttime sky and noticed a slowly moving speck of light, one of the early artificial satellites:

"A satellite!" we said to each other in amazement. Perhaps Echo One or Two? In the wilderness, out of sight or hearing of other men, no light, no town, no highway visible, we were watching a man-made vehicle in space, one of the twentieth century's latest miracles. Toward this, we realized, man headed when he chipped that rough stone tool in Olduvai Gorge. The hand that first formed a tool had now made a rocket to leave the planet. (*ES*, xi)

The image of the artificial satellite passing over the nighttime African wilderness captures the sense of contrast and unity that the *Earth Shine* essays create. It also serves as a striking reminder that the Lindberghs in these essays appear less as voyagers and more as residents. In contrast to the early years and early books, in which Lindbergh recorded her impressions of the unusual and exciting locations and cultures to which their aircraft carried them, now she is recording her impression of other voyagers (the astronauts) who are embarking on their space-age exploratory flights. The Lindbergh perspective in *Earth Shine* is less that of the voyager than that of one who is observing the voyages of others but who can appreciate the value of those voyages.

Chapter Thirteen

The Writings of
Anne Morrow Lindbergh
in Perspective

North to the Orient provides an auspicious beginning to Lindbergh's career. Although she initially despaired of discovering a unified approach to her account of their 1931 trip to the Orient, the personal unhappiness brought on by the death of their infant son provided the key she needed. In her attempt to recapture some of the excitement and exuberance of the year of the trip, she incorporated perception as the motif and the theme of the book. The unity provided by her emphasis upon seeing and understanding also helped to ensure that the book would be appreciably more appealing than many of the other flight narratives appearing at the time. In its blend of style and substance it is one of Lindbergh's most enduring and important achievements. Its lasting popularity is an indication of that success.

The motivation to tell the story of *North to the Orient* partly as a means of reliving valued family experiences also can be seen in *Listen! the Wind,* as Lindbergh focuses primarily upon the frame of mind of two couples, the Porto Praia station manager and his wife, and Lindbergh and her husband. Lindbergh is not as interested in describing the sights of the final third of their 1933 European and African flight as she is in describing its effects on her. In its focus on the interior, emotional aspect of the flight it is more revealing and more innovative than any other of her works. It may be her most successful literary accomplishment, a judgment Saint-Exupéry noted when it first appeared.

Although it is not normally associated with the Lindberghs' flying experiences, *The Wave of the Future* is an indirect product of their air travels, for it is derived from impressions they received during their 1937 and 1938 European flights. The keystone work of Lindbergh's trilogy of noninterventionist essays, *The Wave of the Future* is a pivotal work, for it marks the transition from writer of travel narratives to social philosopher. Attacked in its time for the cautionary note that it sounded, it nevertheless is a milestone document both in Lindbergh's career and in the mood of prewar America.

The transition to an essentially philosophic mode of presentation continues in her study of the mental struggle of Eve Alcott, Lindbergh's thinly disguised representative in *The Steep Ascent*. The terrain over which Alcott and her husband fly from England to Italy is described not from the perspective of the factual geographer but from the viewpoint of a woman who sees the landscape in symbolic terms, and for whom their near approach to disaster in the fog-blocked mountains represents a spiritual rather than a physical crisis. It is likely that Lindbergh chose a fictional mode to tell the story because it would have seemed presumptuous on her part to suggest that she herself had experienced the full range of thoughts attributed to her fictional counterpart. Like *The Wave of the Future*, *The Steep Ascent* represents another important step in her career.

In her postwar writings Lindbergh completes the transition to her preferred mode of expression. The five essays published from 1947 to 1950 describing postwar conditions in Europe affirm her commitment to a belief in international cooperation and understanding that lies at the heart of *The Wave of the Future*. The marked emphasis on spiritual values found in these essays is a fundamental component of her persuasive appeal.

Gift from the Sea firmly establishes Lindbergh as the philosopher of family relationships. Her primary concern in all of her works is to promote understanding in the intimate family, as in *Listen! the Wind* and *Gift from the Sea*, as well as in the extended, or national, family, as in *The Wave of the Future* and her postwar essays. As *Gift from the Sea* illustrates, her belief in the importance of perception, of seeing oneself and one's surroundings clearly, lies at the heart of her creative efforts. *Gift from the Sea* represents the essential Lindbergh, the maker of the meditative essay, her truest form of expression.

The Unicorn and Other Poems provides an alternative form of expression of the Lindbergh philosophy, and the structure of the book illustrates her basic rhetorical approach: engagement ("Love"), conflict ("Death," "Captive Spirit"), analysis ("The Unicorn"), and adjustment ("Open Sky," "Wind of Time"). The poems of *The Unicorn* are individual strands that constitute a fabric of philosophic expression.

Dearly Beloved naturally follows from *The Steep Ascent* and *Gift from the Sea*. Cast in the fictional mode of *The Steep Ascent*, it is a more comfortable method of presenting the typically complex Lindbergh perspective. The multiple narrators of *Dearly Beloved* allow the expression of contrasting and complementing viewpoints on the marital relationship essential to the Lindbergh dialectic. The effect of *The Steep Ascent* suffered, in part, because the abundance of philosophic viewpoints expressed by Eve Alcott was too great a burden for one narrator to bear. The use of multiple narrators in *Dearly Beloved* is a more natural solution to the problem. The family groupings in *Dearly Beloved* illustrate both the intimate and international aspects of Lindbergh's concerns, for the families represent different cultures and different nationalities as well as differing viewpoints on the possibilities of family relationships.

In *Earth Shine* Lindbergh's concept of the human family expands to its ultimate form, as she considers the interrelationships of humans and animals, and life on earth as one large family stretching across history and geographical boundaries. She completes the cycle of her travel narratives in *Earth Shine* as she and her husband remain at home while the century's latest travelers, the astronauts, set out to explore the moon.

Continuity in Diversity

The power of clear and accurate perception is Lindbergh's most consistent and important theme. It is given initial statement in *North to the Orient* and continues in every work through *Earth Shine*. It lies at the heart of her experiences in *Listen! the Wind* and *The Steep Ascent,* and it provides the fundamental basis for discussion in *Gift from the Sea.* Whether she is looking over the side of the aircraft as they fly across the remote areas of Canada or holding a seashell in her hand, her foremost concern is to appreciate the full significance of the objects she is observing.

Linked to her desire for true perception is her interest in natural objects, whether they be seashells, wild animals, or geographic features. For her, every object has a meaning whose importance can be discovered if it is examined properly. Her concern for the well-being of wildlife and her belief in the necessary interaction between humans and animals expressed in *Earth Shine* are a logical development from her interest in understanding the meaning of features of the natural world.

Lindbergh's belief in the inherent value of natural objects is linked to the profound sense of spirituality with which she sees the world.

Beginning in *The Wave of the Future* and continuing through her post-war essays and other later works, her thoughts are consistently of the value of spiritual belief—not religion, necessarily—but of the nature of sensitive introspection that leads to self-assessment of the kind practiced by truly spiritual individuals. The one word that describes such an individual is *saint,* a word that occurs frequently in her writings.

An important aspect of Lindbergh's presentation of themes of perception, the value of the natural world, and spirituality is the pattern of images and symbols through which those themes are most often conveyed. The most important images are those associated with nature—the wind and the sea. The wind is often represented as an antagonistic force that threatens to prevent the successful completion of the journey, as it does in *Listen! the Wind* and a number of the poems. However, the sea and its allied forms—waves, rivers, and streams—are associated with changes and continuities in the flow of life. In *The Wave of the Future* the wave represents a revolutionary change in world cultures, and the ocean in *Gift from the Sea* represents an environment in which personal change is possible and necessary process. In *Dearly Beloved* members of both families are seen as part of a continually flowing stream symbolizing the cyclic pattern of life, marriage, birth, and death.

Another central image in Lindbergh's writing is that of the web or fabric, both constructed of an interwoven network of threads. This image represents the natural interrelationship of various aspects of human life and activity. The fabric serves as the central metaphor of *The Steep Ascent,* while the web is central to *Gift from the Sea* and *Dearly Beloved.* In both *Gift from the Sea* and *Dearly Beloved* the web is linked to the idea of the woman as the center of family activities; this notion is reinforced in the use of a similar image, that of the wheel, in which the woman occupies the unmoving central focus of a variety of family activities.

Lindbergh consistently establishes patterns of contrasts—the old and the new, technology and the natural world, community and isolation, movement and stillness—that create special dynamics within the works. Although her works seem to be models of unhurried, reflective thought, they possess tensions of various kinds that the narrative voice identifies, defines, and then attempts to resolve. Her view—undoubtedly inherited from her father—is that there are no easy solutions to the problems she ponders. Her works do not favor one contrasting value over another, but look for acceptable middle paths, in which the valuable features of the opposing forces can be merged.

Critical Response

Serious literary criticism of Lindbergh's works is practically non-existent. The prevalent form of evaluation is the book review, and too often these reviews have consisted of a brief biographical sketch and a polite summary of the book. Lindbergh appears to have been seen in one of two fashions; either she was given polite acknowledgment as the writing wife of a world-famous aviator, or else she was severely attacked for her ideas or her technique. Beyond the praise of Saint-Exupéry and the disparagement of Ciardi, little else in the way of true critical commentary can be found.

Undoubtedly part of the reason for Lindbergh's critical neglect is due to her unique place in history. As the wife of the century's most widely recognized hero, she was not seen as an individual. Her partnership with Charles Lindbergh marked her as a woman apart from all other women and all other authors. The public eye focused upon her life and her career with an almost unendurable intensity. Her marriage made it impossible for her writings to be read with a detached critical response.

Another likely reason for the lack of critical response is the fact that her writings do not seem to fit comfortably into the normal literary classifications of fiction, essay, and poetry. Her earliest works were travel writings which appeared to recount the adventures of the world's most famous aviator—her husband—and it was not an easy task for the reading public to consider them as an account of her intellectual journey as well. When *The Wave of the Future* became immediately controversial, the response was based on political disagreement and quarrels with Lindbergh's logic, not on consideration of her literary technique. *Gift from the Sea* was typically seen as inspirational writing, not as a variation of the literary essay. Because she almost never produced the same kind of book twice, critics found it difficult to assess each work as it appeared. Only when she published a book resembling a standard literary effort—*The Unicorn and Other Poems*—did the critics feel qualified to assess it, and then only with unhappy results.

The key to appreciating the achievement of Anne Morrow Lindbergh lies in the recognition that her fundamental mode of writing is persuasive and that the point of her writing is to express a way of seeing the world. She is not really to be thought of as a poet or novelist; she is a philosopher at heart. Her philosophic message is the importance of developing a clear perception of self, of others, and of one's surroundings.

Like her two literary mentors, Rilke and Saint-Exupéry, she is not interested in writing poetry or works of fiction as much as in expressing a philosophical viewpoint. Evaluated strictly as fiction, *The Steep Ascent* and *Dearly Beloved* may disappoint some readers, just as *The Unicorn and Other Poems* disappointed others. But Lindbergh's philosophic mode of presentation results in fictional and poetic creations that differ from the norm. Virginia Woolf's *To the Lighthouse* is meant to introduce ambiguities, not resolve them, and T. S. Eliot's view of twentieth-century society in *The Waste Land* works on a literary, not a social, level. To read Lindbergh as part of the mainstream of modern American literature is to read her in an incomplete context. While her philosophical heritage can be traced back to New England transcendentalists like Emerson and Thoreau, who sought to define the self in its relation to natural surroundings, her habit of thought also links her to modern European idealists of the human spirit like Kafka, Koestler, and of course, Rilke and Saint-Exupéry.

Because she was raised and educated in New England, but intimately familiar with European cultures, it was inevitable that Lindbergh should synthesize the two primary influences of her early years in the creation of her literary efforts. It was also inevitable that the unhappy and controversial events of her private and public life should themselves become the central issues of her major works.

Conclusion

The following paragraph, taken from *The Wave of the Future*, serves as an appropriate point of closure for this study of the writings of Anne Morrow Lindbergh, for it conveys the essence of her style, her ideals, her point of view, and her appeal:

The intellectual is constantly betrayed by his own vanity. God-like, he blandly assumes that he can express everything in words; whereas the things one loves, lives, and dies for are not, in the last analysis, words. To write or to speak is almost inevitably to lie a little. It is an attempt to clothe an intangible in a tangible form; to compress an immeasurable into a mold. And in the act of compression, how Truth is mangled and torn! The writer is the eternal Procrustes who must fit his unhappy guests, his ideas, to his set bed of words. (*WF*, 6–7)

Molded by her attraction for the Quaker ideal, her belief in her father's moderation, her commitment to her husband's travel and technical work, and her need to speak out on moral issues of a political or personal nature, Anne Morrow Lindbergh will be remembered for her intense idealism, for her persuasive, rational style, and for the variety of literary creations that carried her voice to millions of readers, not only in America, but in nearly every country in the world.

Selected Bibliography

PRIMARY SOURCES

1. Books

North to the Orient. New York: Harcourt, Brace & Co., 1935. Illustrated with maps by Charles Lindbergh.

Listen! the Wind. New York: Harcourt, Brace & Co., 1938. With foreword and map drawings by Charles Lindbergh.

The Wave of the Future. New York: Harcourt, Brace & Co., 1940.

The Steep Ascent. New York: Harcourt, Brace & Co., 1944.

Gift from the Sea. New York: Pantheon Books, 1955.

The Unicorn and Other Poems. 1935–1955. New York: Pantheon Books, 1956.

Dearly Beloved. New York: Harcourt, Brace & World, 1962.

Earth Shine. New York: Harcourt, Brace & World, 1969.

Bring Me A Unicorn: Diaries and Letters. 1922–1928. New York: Harcourt Brace Jovanovich, 1972.

Hour of Gold. Hour of Lead: Diaries and Letters. 1929–1932. New York: Harcourt Brace Jovanovich, 1973.

Locked Rooms and Open Doors: Diaries and Letters. 1933–1935. New York: Harcourt Brace Jovanovich, 1974.

The Flower and the Nettle: Diaries and Letters. 1936–1939. New York: Harcourt Brace Jovanovich, 1976.

War Within and Without: Diaries and Letters. 1939–1944. New York: Harcourt Brace Jovanovich, 1980.

2. Shorter published works (articles, essays, prefaces, reviews)

"Flying Around the North Atlantic." *National Geographic Magazine* 66 (September 1934):259–337. With a foreword by Charles Lindbergh.

"Adventurous Writing." *Saturday Review of Literature* 20 (14 October 1939):8–9. Review of Antoine de Saint-Exupéry's *Wind. Sand and Stars.*

"Prayer for Peace." *Reader's Digest* 36 (January 1940):1–8.

"Reaffirmation." *Atlantic Monthly* 167 (June 1941):681–86.

"Religion and Politics." *Common Sense* 11 (June 1942):207–9. A review of Aldous Huxley's *Grey Eminence.*

"Wartime Waiting." *Progressive.* 12 July 1943, p. 11. A review of Ann Leighton's *While We Are Absent.*

"The Most Unforgettable Character I've Met." *Reader's Digest* 50 (January 1947):1–4, 171–74. A sketch of the playwright Edward Sheldon.

"The Flame of Europe." *Reader's Digest* 52 (January 1948):141–46.
"One Starts at Zero." *Reader's Digest* 52 (February 1948):73–75.
"Anywhere in Europe." *Harper's Magazine* 196 (April 1948):300–302.
"Airliner to Europe: Notes from a Passenger's Diary." *Harper's Magazine* 197 (September 1948):43–47.
"The Mother and the Child." *Harper's Bazaar* 42 (December 1948):89–90, 156.
"Our Lady of Risk." *Life Magazine* 29 (10 July 1950):80–91.
"As I See our First Lady." *Look Magazine* 28 (19 May 1964):103–8.
"Immersion in Life." *Life Magazine* 61 (21 October 1966):88–98.
"The Heron and the Astronaut." *Life Magazine* 66 (28 February 1969):14–27.
"Harmony with the Life around Us." *Good Housekeeping* 171 (July 1970):62, 150–53. Text of Smith College address.
"The Journey Not Taken." *Good Housekeeping* 179 (July 1978):50–53. Text of Smith College address.
Introduction to *Antoine de Saint-Exupéry, Wartime Writings, 1939–1944.* New York: Harcourt Brace Jovanovich, 1986, ix–xvii.

3. Poetry
Those poems which were collected in *The Unicorn and Other Poems* are marked with an asterisk (*).

"Height." *Scribner's Magazine* 83 (April 1928):409.
Four Poems. *Literary Digest* 100 (9 March 1929):38, 43, 46. Contains texts of four poems written during Smith College days: "Caprice," "Unicorn," "A Certain Woman," "A Letter with a Foreign Stamp."
"Remembrance." *Literary Digest* 100 (16 March 1929):29. Another poem written at Smith College.
*"No Harvest Ripening." *Saturday Review* 21 (18 November 1939):10.
*"Security." *Saturday Review* 21 (16 December 1939):8.
Three poems. *Atlantic Monthly* 165 (April 1940):456–57: *"Visitation," *"Elegy under the Stars," and *"Alms."
Two Poems. *Atlantic Monthly* 167 (March 1941):338–39: *"Testament," *"A Final Cry."
Three "Songs for Flying." *Atlantic Monthly* 180 (July 1947):36: "Growing Up," "The Trolls," *"Closing In.'"
"Two Poems for November." *Atlantic Monthly* 180 (November 1947):122: *"All Saints' Day," *"Burning Tree."
*"Second Sowing." *Atlantic Monthly* 182 (August 1948):70.
*"Winter Tree." *Atlantic Monthly* 185 (March 1950):46.
*"Man and the Child." *Atlantic Monthly* 187 (February 1951):29.
*"Within the Wave." *Atlantic Monthly* 188 (October 1951):38.
*"Space." *Atlantic Monthly* 188 (November 1951):35.
*"Stone." *Atlantic Monthly* 189 (January 1952):44.
*"A Leaf, a Flower, and a Stone." *Atlantic Monthly* 190 (October, 1952):52.

*"Broken Shell." *Atlantic Monthly* 193 (January 1954):64.
*"Back to the Islands." *Atlantic Monthly* 193 (March 1954):66.
*"Bare Tree." *Atlantic Monthly* 195 (March, 1955):56.
*"Two Citadels." *Ladies Home Journal* 73 (August 1956):120.
*"Even." *Ladies Home Journal* 73 (September 1956):14.
*"Revisitation" and other poems. *Vogue* 128 (15 September 1956):122–23.
*"Dogwood." *Ladies Home Journal* 73 (October 1956):110.
"Mid-summer." *Atlantic Monthly* 200 (December 1957):44.

4. Manuscripts
The bulk of the Lindbergh family papers is in the Sterling Memorial Library of Yale University. At the present time these papers are not available to the public. However, a substantial number of papers and manuscripts are available in the Sophia Smith Collection in the library of Smith College, including Lindbergh's Smith College literary efforts. Some articles and photographs about Charles and Anne Lindbergh are in the archives of the library of the National Air and Space Museum in Washington, D. C.

SECONDARY SOURCES

The following entries offer the most insightful assessment or provide helpful background information about the author or her individual works.

Ciardi, John. "A Close Look at the Unicorn." *Saturday Review* 40 (12 January 1957):54–57. A scathing review of *The Unicorn and Other Poems*.
Ciardi, John. "The Reviewer's Duty to Damn." *Saturday Review* 40 (16 February 1957):24–25, 54–55. Ciardi's spirited response to the majority of *Saturday Review* readers who were outraged by his original review of *The Unicorn*.
Cole, Wayne S. *Charles A. Lindbergh and the Battle Against American Intervention*. New York: Harcourt Brace Jovanovich, 1974. Provides good discussion of Charles Lindbergh's isolationist activities from 1939 through 1941; also contains some discussion of Anne Morrow Lindbergh's activities during the same period.
Cousins, Norman. "John Ciardi and the Readers." *Saturday Review* 40 (16 February 1957):22–23. Cousins' attempt to distance *Saturday Review's* editorial policy from Ciardi's criticism of Lindbergh's *The Unicorn*.
"Dear Mrs. Lindbergh." *Life Magazine* 39 (3 October 1955):118–27. A review of the reactions of several women from across America to the messages in *Gift from the Sea*. Contains pictures and comments of the women, most of whom describe themselves as largely frustrated in their attempts

to achieve the kind of intellectual and spiritual satisfaction described in
Gift from the Sea.

Eisenhower, Julie Nixon. "Anne Morrow Lindbergh." A chapter in Eisenhower's *Special People,* 121–50. New York: Simon and Schuster, 1977. An especially revealing account of the Lindbergh marriage.

Friedrich, Carl Joachim. "We Build the Future." *Atlantic Monthly* 167 (January 1941):33–35. An opposing response to *The Wave of the Future.*

Lindbergh, Charles. *The Wartime Journals of Charles A. Lindbergh.* New York: Harcourt Brace Jovanovich, 1970. Contains Lindbergh's diary entries from March 1938 through June 1945; material helps to illuminate Anne Morrow Lindbergh's diaries and letters during that period (*The Flower and the Nettle; War Within and Without*).

Mosley, Leonard. *Lindbergh: A Biography.* New York: Doubleday, 1976. The most detailed biography so far written about Charles Lindbergh; contains some information about Anne Morrow Lindbergh.

Nicolson, Harold. *Dwight Morrow: A Biography.* New York: Harcourt, Brace & Co., 1935. Provides the most complete account of Anne Morrow Lindbergh's father. Nicolson's biography is irritatingly patronizing at times, but is good on Morrow's diplomatic successes. Lindbergh contributed a touching account of her family at breakfast, which Nicolson included (160–63).

Patterson, Jean Rushmore. *Letter to Anne Lindbergh from Jean Rushmore Patterson.* New York: Lenox Hill Press, 1940. A Lindbergh-like rebuttal to *The Wave of the Future.*

Richart, Bette. "Since Sappho." *Commonweal* 64 (7 September 1956):568–70. A disparaging review of *The Unicorn and Other Poems.*

Ross, Walter S. *The Last Hero: Charles A. Lindbergh.* New York: Harper & Row, 1968. An early and informal biography of Charles Lindbergh containing some information on Anne Morrow Lindbergh.

Saint-Exupéry, Antoine de. "A Fertile Anguish." In his *A Sense of Life,* 167–77. New York: Funk & Wagnalls, 1965. Originally published as an introduction to the French edition of *Listen! the Wind,* this early (1939) review of Lindbergh's work remains one of the most sensitive and perceptive to date.

Weeks, Edward. *Writers and Friends.* Boston: Little Brown & Co., 1981, 30–33. Some kind words from a sympathetic editor.

White, E. B. "One Man's Meat." *Harper's* 182 (February 1941):329–32. Probably the most thoughtful review of *The Wave of the Future.*

Whitman, Alden. "A Conversation with Anne Morrow Lindbergh." *Ladies Home Journal* 93 (May 1976):68–70, 179–86. Chatty and informal discussion with Lindbergh; more on life than writings.

Whitman, Alden. "Anne Morrow Lindbergh Reminisces about 'Life with Lindy.'" *New York Times Magazine,* 8 May 1977, pp. 16–28. Biographical overview.

Index